British Library Occasional Papers 2

Library Publishing

British Library Occasional Papers 2

Library Publishing

Report of a seminar
held at the British Library
11–13 April 1983

Edited by David Way

The British Library 1985

© 1985 The Contributors

Published by
The British Library
Reference Division Publications
Great Russell Street
London WC1B 3DG

and 51 Washington Street,
Dover, New Hampshire 03820

British Library Cataloguing in Publication Data

Library publishing: report of a seminar held at
   the British Library, 11–13 April 1983.—British
   Library occasional papers; 2)
   1. Library publications—Great Britain
   I. Way, David, *1957*– II. British Library
   III. Series
   070.5'94 Z716.6

ISBN 0-7123-0040-6

Designed by Alan Bartram
Typeset in Linotron 202 Bembo by Channel Eight Typesetters Ltd,
Bexhill-on-Sea
Printed in England by Adlard and Son Ltd, Dorking

Contents

Editor's preface	David Way	vii
List of participants		viii
Introductory session		xi
Publishing policy	Hugh Cobbe	1
Operating a publishing company	Michael Hoare	9
Discussion		
Operating a publishing department	Robert Cross	15
Discussion		
Production techniques for short-run reference books	John Mitchell	21
Discussion		
Marketing (1)	Alec Bolton	27
Marketing (2)	Jane Carr	31
Discussion		
Retailing in on-site bookshops	Heather Dean	39
Discussion		
Operating a publishing programme through outside agencies	Dana Pratt	45
Operating a microform publishing programme	Kenneth Carpenter	47
Discussion		
Operating a translation journal publishing programme	Peter Haigh	55
Publishing and preservation	Nicolas Barker	57
Discussion		

Aspects of new technology	Hugh Pinnock	63
Discussion		
Electronic publishing	David Martin	69
Discussion		
Summing-up	Hugh Cobbe	75
Discussion: a summary		79

Editor's preface
David Way

This seminar, held at the British Library in London on 11–13 April 1983, brought together representatives of many of the major research libraries to discuss a wide range of topics related to the theme of library publishing. The seminar also proved to be an inaugural meeting, for it was decided that the group could profitably meet again on a regular basis; the International Group of Publishing Libraries has therefore been set up, with the intention of assembling biennially to share experience and explore the possibilities of active collaboration between libraries which operate publishing programmes.

The seminar was initiated and organised by Hugh Cobbe, Head of Publications in the British Library Reference Division, and chaired jointly by him and Dana Pratt, Director of Publishing at the Library of Congress. To both, to all who assisted in the smooth running of the seminar, and to all participants, grateful thanks are due. Thanks, too, to Sir Harry Hookway, Chief Executive of the British Library at the time, for his welcoming speech; to Alex Wilson, Director General, British Library Reference Division, for his active support and for hosting a reception on the final evening; and to Gordon Graham, Chairman of Butterworth and Co (Publishers) Ltd, for his memorable speech at the closing dinner.

This report is the product of long hours at the word-processor (the joys and perils of which might usefully form the subject of a session at a future IGPL seminar), and is in many ways a recreation of what took place rather than a comprehensive and verbatim record. A few papers were presented in typescript form, and these are here presented unaltered. The majority of papers, however, and all of the discussion, have had to be brought back to life from my own notes – with the consequence that my efforts to produce a readable text may have resulted in some degree of misreporting. I take responsibility for any errors of transmission which have been unwittingly introduced, and ask forgiveness of any who consider that they have been misrepresented.

I should like to thank all who have encouraged me in this labour-intensive method of production and who have waited so patiently for the result, in particular my colleagues Jane Carr and John Mitchell. My greatest debt of gratitude is to Hugh Cobbe, who has had to wait more patiently than anyone; this is his book.

List of participants

Nicolas Barker	Head of Conservation, The British Library
Alec T Bolton	Director of Publishing, National Library of Australia
Mgr Paul Canart	Biblioteca Apostolica Vaticana, Rome
Kenneth E Carpenter	Research and Publications Librarian, Harvard University Libraries
Jane Carr	Marketing Officer, Reference Division Publications, The British Library
Hugh Cobbe	Head of Publications, British Library Reference Division
Robert Cross	Head of Publications, British Museum (Natural History)
Dr Karl Dachs	Keeper of Manuscripts, Bayerische Staatsbibliothek
Heather Dean	Marketing Manager, British Museum Publications Ltd
Joanna Dodsworth	Publications Officer, The Bodleian Library, Oxford
Charles Ellis	Managing Director, Library Association Publishing
Gwynneth Evans	Executive Secretary, National Library of Canada
Dr Clive Field	John Rylands University Library, Manchester
Ian Gibb	Keeper of Special Printed Materials, British Library Reference Division
Rachael Goldstein	Columbia University Libraries, New York

Stephen Green	Head, Newspaper Library, The British Library
Dr Geraint Gryffydd	Librarian, National Library of Wales
Peter Haigh	Head of Publications, British Library Lending Division
David J Hall	Under Librarian (Administration), Cambridge University Library
Michael Hoare	Managing Director, British Museum Publications Ltd
Marie E Korey	Head of Rare Book Department, Free Library of Philadelphia
David Martin	Director of Automated Services, Bibliographic Services Division, The British Library
Dr Ann Matheson	National Library of Scotland
John Mitchell	Production Consultant, Reference Division Publications, The British Library
Professor Dr Gunther Pflug	Director, Deutsche Bibliothek, Frankfurt-am-Main
Dr Hugh Pinnock	Research and Development Department, The British Library
Dana J Pratt	Director of Publishing, Library of Congress
Nancy M Shea	Clark Memorial Library, Los Angeles
Ruth Ann Stewart	Associate Director for External Services, New York Public Library

Margaret Treen	Head of Press and Public Relations, The British Library
David Way	Publications Editor, Reference Division Publications, The British Library
Dr A W Willemsen	Deputy Librarian, The Royal Library, The Hague
Thomas F Wright	Librarian, Clark Memorial Library, Los Angeles

Introductory Session

A member of each institution represented at the seminar was asked to give the meeting a résumé of its publishing activities.

National Library of Australia (Mr Alec Bolton)

Publications is a small branch of the National Library of Australia, with a staff of eleven out of the institution's total of 650. The branch is responsible for the production of about 120 issued publications a year, ranging from major bibliographical works, issued fortnightly, to unpriced pamphlets and brochures describing the services and collections of the Library.

In giving the following figures, I should point out that the recently devalued Australian dollar is worth about 59 English pence, and 86 US cents.

In the last completed financial year, to the end of June 1982, the branch had a production budget of $428,000 out of the Library's total budget of $18.2 M. No part of the amount was deductible for salaries and overheads. Expenditure on production actually totalled $419,000.

Cash revenue from the sale of publications in the same financial year was $471,000, and the value of priced publications given to other libraries under exchange arrangements was $90,000. There is an overall objective to recover all externally incurred costs of production.

There are two parts to the publishing programme. The major part consists of bibliographical and service publications directed mostly to the community of other libraries. Many of these are published in fulfilment of responsibilities under an Act of Parliament. Most of such publications are printed, but there is an increasing number on COM fiche.

The minor part of the programme consists of a small output of more general publications based on materials in the Library's collections, and intended to make particular treasures of the collections available to the public. Publications in the trade programme are distributed through booksellers and other retailers. The general or trade programme has been in existence since 1972. So far it has consisted only of material in printed form, but we are contemplating the publication of sound recordings from the archives of the Sound Recordings Collection, and video recordings from the National Film Archive. Prints and postcards and other publications (such as diaries) all form part of the programme.

Some editorial and design work is contracted out. In-house editorial tasks are performed by one editor and myself. We have a production manager who is also the administrative officer of the Publications Branch, and we have five members of staff who are concerned with the warehousing, invoicing and despatch of publications, and the maintenance of subscription records and mailing lists. Invoicing and stock control are still carried on by manual procedures, but mailing lists are automated in the Library's main computer. The computer is also used as a word processor for the generation of many publications.

The National Library building is a tourist attraction of Canberra, and has about 350,000 casual visitors a year, many of them schoolchildren. The Publications Branch maintains a small print shop in the Library foyer, where the full range of Library publications is available for sale. In the last financial year the shop had a turnover of $87,000, or 20 per cent of the total revenue. The shop is staffed by two part-time workers and is open seven days a week. It is not a general bookshop, and carries only material originated by the Library or relating to loan exhibitions.

Biblioteca Apostolica Vaticana, Rome (Mgr Paul Canart)

The Library forms part of the Vatican Museums and its collections contain manuscripts, printed books and stamps. The policy of the Library is to put its treasures at the disposal of scholars, and to this end over 50 volumes of catalogues of manuscripts have been produced, along with specialised catalogues of classical manuscripts, and exhibition catalogues (24 so far). There is an ambitious programme of facsimile publishing, undertaken both by the Library itself and in cooperation with other publishers (for example, Belser of Stuttgart). Collections of archive documents ('documents' here taken to mean maps, seals, drawings, coins etc, as well as manuscripts), and editions of texts, mainly concerning the history of the Papacy, have been published. There is an extensive microfilming programme.

In 1982, 13 titles were published, and currently there are 16 titles in production. Library publications are sold on a self-financing basis. Three or four local printers are regularly used. The Prefect of the Library is himself responsible for publishing policy and implementation, along with the Keepers of the collections. There are no full-time publishing staff.

Harvard University Libraries (Mr Kenneth Carpenter)

There is a collection of libraries scattered around Harvard University and Mr

Carpenter's role is to coordinate their publishing activities and to represent the University in negotiations with outside publishers wanting to draw upon its resources. There is little publishing done internally, beyond the quarterly Harvard Library Bulletin and guides to the collections (for example, the Directory of Manuscript Collections). However, there has been a great deal of microform publishing in the past few years, done by outside publishers and controlled by Mr Carpenter.

British Museum (Natural History) (Mr Robert Cross)

The British Museum (Natural History) is a major taxonomic research institute, with some 370 scientists on its staff. It has a very large library, which includes among its holdings more than 30,000 pieces of artwork.

The publishing operation has three components:

1. Publication of scholarly research, in bulletins and in monographs. Four different Bulletins are published (totalling 60 parts a year, sold on annual subscription), requiring an investment of £140,000 pa. Well over half the work on these is performed outside the Museum. Approximately six monographs a year are published, either typeset, photographed from camera-ready copy or put onto microfiche.

2. Popular/educational publications. These are designed to produce profit, and, as well as books, the programme includes prints, postcards, models etc (all checked and approved by the scientific departments). The investment is about £200,000 pa.

3. Retail outlets. There are two shops on the main South Kensington site, and two on a second site (at Tring, Hertfordshire). Each has a manager, and they aim to be profitable.

The publishing operation is expected to be self-financing. The salaries of staff involved have to be paid back to the Museum (the current salary bill is running at about £320,000 pa). The scholarly publishing has now been separated out, however, and is not expected to be profitable.

(Hugh Cobbe commented that this function of being on hand to publish for the parent institution's staff, in several different forms, was probably common to all present.)

Bayerische Staatsbibliothek, Munich (Dr Karl Dachs)

The current and planned publishing activities of the Bayerische Staatsbibliothek cover three areas:

1. Publication of catalogues of library holdings: manuscript catalogues, the catalogue of incunabula, an inventory of 16th-century printed books published in the German language area (as one part of a retrospective German National Bibliography), a catalogue of printed music, and a short title catalogue for the Library's printed books from 1501–1840.

2. Exhibition catalogues.

3. Facsimile editions of valuable manuscripts and colour postcards.

Only on rare occasions does the Library act as its own publisher; the budget allocations for publications are small and the proceeds from our own publications cannot be used for further publications but rather must be handed over to the State Treasury. Therefore, it is the Library's policy to obtain well-known publishers for its publications. We consciously do not do all our work with one publisher, in order to avoid becoming too dependent upon him. Rather, each project is proposed to three publishing houses, in order to create competition so that the Library can negotiate the most favourable terms that can be obtained.

In practice, the following three procedures are developed:

1. The publisher takes on the production and distribution of the work at his own cost and at his own risk. The Library delivers at no charge the manuscript and the originals for the purposes of illustration, and as compensation receives voucher copies. This practice is applied to catalogues of holdings and facsimile editions.

2. The procedure is similar for exhibition catalogues, although in this case the Library takes charge of sales during the exhibition, on commission and at a reduced price, and often guarantees sales, for example of 1,000 copies.

3. In the case of publications for which only a small number of customers can be anticipated, for example manuscript catalogues or exhibition catalogues with a narrowly defined and highly specialised topic, the Library contributes a non-redeemable subsidy (of around 5,000 to 10,000 DM).

There exists a very close collaboration between the Library and the given publishing houses. The Library will usually not only deliver the manuscript and illustration originals and take charge of proof-reading, but it also has considerable influence over the outward appearance of the work.

(Mr Hugh Cobbe commented that the close relationship which the Staatsbibliothek had with publishers was perhaps symptomatic of the well-developed publishing industry in West Germany. In other countries it would not be so easy to establish such relationships. Dr Dachs agreed and commented that there were at least five West German publishers who specialised in library publishing.)

Bodleian Library, Oxford (Ms Joanna Dodsworth)

Up until about ten years ago, all the Bodleian publishing was handled by Oxford University Press, who had to charge at commercial rates. Joanna Dodsworth was appointed Publications Officer three years ago and her responsibilities embrace in-house printing, management of sales points, filmstrip and slide production, as well as book, booklet and postcard publishing. There are four part-time shop staff and two clerks who deal with the filmstrips and slides. With 800,000 visitors a year, the need for a purpose-built shop is proving acute.

Publishing is undertaken on a small scale. The main regular item is the *Bodleian Library Record*. Postcards, guidebooks, exhibition catalogues and small picture-books (nothing that would require a large investment) are produced. When larger projects are planned, these have to be as joint ventures with commerical publishers (for example, two large catalogues are coming out with OUP this year – each was negotiated separately). Microform publishers and facsimile publishers are negotiated with, the Library usually obtaining a royalty and free copies of the publications that result. Some outside funds are tapped for particular projects – for example, the University, the British Academy and the British Library Research and Development fund. Small publications are expected to show profit. It is hoped that a proper publishing department might be established in the future.

(Ms Dodsworth was asked if there was any difference between the publishing programme now and as it was before when under the aegis of OUP, and she replied that there was now a trend towards more general publications. A problem was that the Library had been suffering acute staff shortages, and as a consequence of their greater level of duties it was becoming very difficult to get staff who 'had books in them' actually to produce. Hugh Cobbe added the general point that it was a fundamental necessity for all those present to have colleagues on the library staff who were enthusiastic about publishing.)

Library Association Publishing (Mr Charles Ellis)

The Library Association, which is the professional association for librarians in the UK and has no public funding, has 80 years of publishing behind it. It has always taken on projects which other publishers believed were not commercially viable, including monographs, catalogues, and, most important, the *Periodical Index* series (now expanded into a monthly *Technology Index* and a quarterly *Humanities Index*). *Library and Information Science Extracts* is probably its best known publication. It also publishes many textbooks in library science.

Half of the LA's staff work in publishing and three-fifths of its income is derived from this source. The need to make a profit has therefore always been present, but this need was considerably sharpened in the 1970s, when the LA faced a rapid escalation in costs. Now Library Association Publishing operates as a limited-liability company, a wholly-owned subsidiary of the LA. It is the largest library science publisher in the UK, having purchased Clive Bingley Ltd in 1980. It also distributes for K G Saur.

National Library of Canada (Mrs Gwynneth Evans)

There are two separate parts of the NLC publishing programme. First, there are mandatory publications, such as the Library's Annual Report and *Canadiana* (the cumulative monthly national bibliography). Secondly, there are discretionary publications, which include bibliographies, union lists, surveys, interlibrary loan data, exhibition catalogues. There is also a programme of thesis dissemination in which 33 Canadian universities are participants; the theses are made available in microform and are sold or can be borrowed on interlibrary loan. Theses are not available in hard copy.

The NLC publications have to be published simultaneously in French and English, which does not help unit costs and can also present a design challenge. Some publications are produced in both hard copy and microform, but increasingly microform is becoming the standard medium for any publication that is subject to regular updating or is cumulative.

NLC publishing policy is administered through the Ministry of Supply and Services. They put out the contracts to printers, handle the distribution and marketing, and fix the prices (a cost factor × 6 mark-up is imposed, except for microform). The NLC relies on the Ministry to take over all publishing functions, having itself produced the original copy (the publications staff of eight includes five editors, and all work up to and including preparation of camera-ready copy is handled in-house). Equally, the NLC does not benefit in direct financial terms from its 'bestsellers'.

(Hugh Cobbe commented that the unusual aspect to NLC operations was its thesis-publishing and he asked if there were any copyright problems. Mrs Evans replied that there were no problems; publishing in this way was taken to constitute 'fair use'. Mr Peter Haigh said that the same applied to theses made available by the British Library Lending Division.)

John Rylands University Library, Manchester
(Dr Clive Field)

The John Rylands Library supports a fairly extensive publishing programme, the major impetus deriving from the original Library which was an independent institution from its opening in 1900 to its incorporation as the Rare Books and Manuscripts Division of the University Library in 1972. Library publications may be divided into four principal categories.

1. Scholarly research publications. The most important of these is the *Bulletin of the John Rylands University Library of Manchester,* a journal for the humanities, which has been published twice yearly since 1903. Besides details of Library accessions and news, each 250-page issue contains an average of ten learned articles which are either the texts of lectures given at the Library or accounts of research by scholars who have used the Library's collections. The *Bulletin* has a net circulation of about 900 copies, of which approximately half are paid for on subscription and half exchanged for equivalent publications worldwide. Reprint rights have been sold to Kraus. About 100 offprints of each article are also produced for sale on a casual basis.

2. Handlists and research tools. A substantial number of handlists or catalogues, preponderately of manuscript collections, have been prepared, mostly by the Library's own staff but occasionally by University academics. About 20–30 of these, dealing with western and oriental manuscripts of the ancient and medieval periods, have been professionally printed, but many more have been produced as duplicated typescript for more limited circulation on and off campus. A growing need to list collections for more recent times is being felt, and a major project, now underway, is for a comprehensive calendar of the papers of Field Marshal Sir Claud Auchinleck.

3. Reader instructional literature. A mass of short and long run instructional literature is produced for, with certain exceptions (for example, the list of current periodicals, for which a charge is made), free dissemination to the Library's more than 30,000 registered readers. The majority is produced in-house, either by offset or photocopying methods – although a general pamphlet guide to the entire Library and a guide to the law collections have been printed more formally. Experiments are now in hand to improve the format and flow of these materials consistent with the need for economy. The use of an instructional videotape since October 1982 undoubtedly renders some of this paper output redundant.

4. Promotional materials. These are designed to introduce the work of the Library to a wider audience. Besides a 28-page colour brochure describing the history and collections of the Library, a wide range of exhibition catalogues, postcards and Christmas cards have also been produced.

With the exception of instructional literature, available from the various Library information desks, distribution of Library publications is undertaken by the Audio-Visual Services Office in the Main Library building and by the general service counter in the Rare Books and Manuscripts Division. Improved marketing and turnover of existing stock is a major priority in the current economic climate, and this is being examined as a matter of urgency.

Columbia University Libraries, New York
(Ms Rachael Goldstein)

Columbia University Libraries have no separate publications department; publications are handled by a branch of user-services division. Printed catalogues have been made available through G K Hall (for example, catalogues of the law library and social work library), but these have not produced much return. Future supplements would probably be handled on a different basis. The Avery Index (an index to the Avery Collection of architectural books) has also been published by G K Hall, based on the Library's card-index. Now the Index is stored on-line, rather than on cards, and when G K Hall wish to do a supplement, the data will be supplied to them on tape. The Library has recently received a Mellon Foundation grant in order to produce a videodisc index of the drawings collection in the Avery Library. The project, shortly to commence, is seen primarily as a preservation function, but the videodisc might eventually be made available for sale.

National Library of Wales (Dr Geraint Gryffyd)

The Library has a small in-house printing unit, employing five people, which has been established for many years and has a fine craft tradition. It is mainly used for internal work, in particular the Library's Annual Report (important for providing details of new acquisitions, which often would not get catalogued for some time) and the *National Library of Wales Journal* (twice-yearly), exhibition catalogues, editions of documents and manuscripts, and occasional monographs. This unit is now under review, and is at present concentrating on three main areas:

1. Bibliographies. A new Bibliography of Wales, amalgamating two previous bibliographies. 2. Reproductions of manuscripts and historical texts. 3. Fundamental works of scholarship of an ancillary nature (for example, the recently-issued 18 volumes of genealogical tables) for which it would be difficult or impossible to find an outside publisher.

(Hugh Cobbe commented that this showed that libraries could – and indeed should – fill publishing gaps.)

British Library Lending Division (Mr Peter Haigh)

The prime functions of BLLD were to provide loan and photocopying services – which it does on a very large scale – and publishing is a minor part of the whole operation, employing some ten people out of a total of over 700. Its publishing has three components:

1. Publications arising from the Division's own stock and specialist materials, and making use of the records already generated as part of the general services, mostly serials. The revenue produced – in the region of £450,000 pa – makes this an important part of the operation. A limited number of monographs (often undertaken in collaboration with outside publishers) is also produced.

2. Acting as a distributor for the *Cumulative Index Medicus* to institutions in the UK, dealing directly with the National Library of Medicine in the USA.

3. Producing cover-to-cover translations of ten Russian scientific journals, in conjunction with several learned institutions. This is a major revenue-earner for the Library. (See p. 55.)

Cambridge University Library (Mr David Hall)

The Library's publishing activities are small-scale, but complicated. There are 53 titles in print, not including some (such as guides to exhibitions) that do not make it onto the publications list. Publications were originally handled by Cambridge University Press, but they came to lose interest in such slow-selling titles, and in jobbing printing too. An in-house printing unit was therefore established, and the Library started to publish on its own account. Stocks of books came back from the CUP warehouse. Now the wheel has turned full circle; CUP sell 15 of the Library's 53 titles on a commission basis, and the Library has the benefit of reaching the 50,000 potential customers who are recipients of the CUP catalogues.

Currently, titles in production include: a Japanese catalogue produced by the University Oriental faculty, jointly sponsored by the University and Library, and to be published by CUP; a major series of catalogues of Hebrew fragments, again to be published by CUP, but on a royalty basis (the Library is providing camera-ready copy); a reprint, by Kraus, of a 19th-century catalogue of the manuscripts, in return for a royalty. The Library is taking tentative steps towards microform publishing; recently, a fiche supplement of new acquisitions has been issued, and the bulky base list of this would also be brought out on fiche, at one-sixth of the hard-copy cost.

The publications fund is run on a self-financing basis, with no injections of money for special projects.

British Museum Publications Ltd (Mr Michael Hoare)

British Museum Publications was set up as a limited-liability company in 1973, wholly-owned by the Trustees of the Museum but not actually part of the Museum. As such, it has no public funding, and must pay all its own overhead costs. It has an obligation to publish anything that the Trustees wish to have published. BMP currently produces about 30–40 titles a year, and has a backlist of about 700 titles. The list ranges from scholarly monographs to popular publications with book club potential, from exhibition catalogues to slides and calendars. There is also a growing list of replicas of items on display in the Museum. Apart from sales points set up at special exhibitions, there are three sales areas (two in the main building and one at the Museum of Mankind, the ethnography department of the Museum), and BMP depends to a large extent on the revenue produced by these shops (which stock books and other merchandise from a wide range of publishers and suppliers) in order to fund its more non-commercial publications.

The company employs about 40 staff, including the shop staff; it has four in-house editors and two production personnel, but all design work is put outside to freelance designers.

Library Company of Philadelphia (*speaker:* Marie E Korey)

Publishing is carried out on a very informal basis, and there are no specialist staff to handle it. Marie Korey, when Curator of Printed Books, was in charge of publications and did a fair amount of the editorial work herself. Typical publications are the Annual Report (written in narrative style), exhibition catalogues, and the occasional facsimile. Certainly the most complex publication produced by the Library was the 'Quarter of a Millenium' exhibition catalogue, which celebrated 250 years' history of the Library Company. The actual production of titles is handled outside the Library. While almost all publications are issued by the Library itself, there are occasional collaborative ventures, for example with G K Hall, and with other Philadelphia institutions. Publications are seen as a means of making the Library better known to the public. Funding is produced on an *ad hoc* basis, with it becoming increasingly necessary for subsidies to be raised before any major project is undertaken.

Free Library of Philadelphia (Marie E Korey)

There are no publications staff, although the Library does have a graphic services office which handles the production of leaflets and brochures. The rare book department has produced catalogues of its holdings and exhibition catalogues, but there is now a need to evaluate what publications ought to be produced and to investigate ways of generating income. There is no publications fund as such. Kraus pay a small royalty on a microform edition of the catalogue of the collections of children's books.

British Library Research and Development Department
(Dr Hugh Pinnock)

The BLRDD produces a number of different publications, all of which arise from the programmes of research which it either itself carries out or which it sponsors. Typical of its projects are those relating to public library research and to library user research. There is a twice-yearly Newsletter, which disseminates current information on new and continuing projects and lists new grants that have been awarded. Final reports on research are made available, and a priced series, Library and Information Research Reports, has recently been initiated, with some good sales resulting. These 'user-friendly' reports are produced and distributed by the British Library Lending Division, and the return is shared between the two divisions. The series of reports is available both in hard copy and microfiche.

Library of Congress (Mr Dana J Pratt)

The Library of Congress started publishing in 1801 (its first title was a book-list, of which a facsimile has recently been produced) and it now issues about 25–30 titles a year. The Publications Office has a staff of eleven, handling all editorial functions but going to outside freelancers for design work. Publications range from scholarly catalogues and bibliographies of the Library collections to exhibition catalogues, postcards, replicas and even ties. There is also a continuing series of editions of the letters of the original founders of Congress. The Library collaborates with outside publishers, and, in the case of many exhibitions and their catalogues, with outside funding agencies and sponsors. On the whole, however, it is funded by taxpayers' money, and the Library is therefore obliged to operate through the Government Printing Office for its production and distribution functions. This inevitably leads to a certain amount of time being spent in negotiations.

British Library Bibliographic Services Division
(Mr David Martin)

The BL Bibliographic Services Division publishes in four media:
1. The *British National Bibliography* is produced in hard copy and in microfiche.

2. *Books in English,* the bi-monthly cumulative bibliography compiled from MARC sources in the UK and USA, is, along with other catalogues, produced on microfiche.

3. Parts of the *British National Bibliography* are made available on magnetic tape.

4. An on-line retrieval system gives access to a number of files, centred on the *BNB* and MARC files, but now being extended to include a wider range of files from both inside and outside the BL.

Clark Memorial Library, Los Angeles (Mr Thomas Wright)

Publications issued by the Clark are conceived of as publicity, and so far have not produced any profit. There is an editorial staff of two. There has recently been a move to use microcomputers for typesetting, in cooperation with a local printer, but as yet this had not produced significant cost-saving.

Publications include:

1. The Augustan Reprint Series of facsimiles of works of the 17th and 18th centuries.

2. Clark Seminar Papers. These are the product of lectures given at the Clark, usually on a particular theme (for example, 'the history of science'), and of a quasi-scholarly, quasi-popular nature. Print-runs are usually 2,000, and they sell at a rate of 500–600 a year.

3. One exhibition catalogue – on the Clark's Dryden collection.

4. A newsletter.

5. An annual volume, produced by California University Press, and subsidised (by $5,000) by the Clark.

6. A catalogue, available through G K Hall.

The Clark is also the home of the California edition of the Works of John Dryden. Future plans include the development of a journal.

New York Public Library (Ruth Ann Stewart)

The NYPL has produced the *Bulletin of Research in the Humanities* (previously the

Bulletin of The New York Public Library) for many years, and this has a circulation of some 700. It has also produced many monographs, facsimiles, and collected letters, all based on the Library holdings. The publications programme used to be publicly funded, but in the mid-1970s the NYPL had to raise funds and the publications staff was reduced. At that time Readex Books took over as publisher and distributor for the NYPL, with editorial and design work controlled by the Library. This arrangement went on until 1982, when the NYPL returned to being its own publisher, buying back the stock.

The NYPL is now looking to expand into trade areas, in order to subsidise the scholarly publications; it is seeking subsidies for specific projects; and it is collaborating with outside publishers (for example Thames and Hudson, and possibly also OUP and Doubleday). A major exhibition programme is planned for 1985, with the opening up of a new area within the Library, so this will entail the setting up of shops and some tied-in publishing. Among other things, the shops will stock postcards, posters and calendars, all produced under licence. In addition the Metropolitan Museum has provided advice in exploring the NYPL collections for products that could be merchandised. A major problem is that the NYPL has had a non-publishing library staff since the 1960s, so that a lot of work is having to be put in to generate new projects.

A reprint programme, in association with the Library's conservation department, is underway. The NYPL is also currently actively involved in discussions with microform publishers.

Royal Library, The Hague, Netherlands (Dr A W Willemsen)

The Royal Library had 'blundered into publishing'; there had been a good deal of improvisation, and little long-term planning. No special staff were employed. Specialist catalogue publishing had always been a tradition, and it was now being undertaken on a large scale. The Royal Library had taken over responsibility for the *Dutch National Bibliography,* and this was an expanding area for development. Publishing is undertaken on the Library's own account, or in association with (or sometimes as a cover for) other institutions. Co-publication with commercial publishers also occurs (for example, the *Dutch National Bibliography,* on which a 20 per cent royalty is received).

The Royal Library has made an arrangement to bypass the Government Printing Office, although the latter did retain a small degree of control.

A cooperative agreement was due to be signed on 22 April 1983 by the Royal Library and seven other bodies, together with four bilateral contracts, the aim being to strengthen and coordinate all activities relating to the *Dutch National Bibliography*, to formulate future publishing policy, and control all resultant by-products. The first step to be taken as a result is the publication of a weekly bibliographical record, drawing upon the Library's own lists.

British Library, Reference Division Publications
(Mr Hugh Cobbe)

The Publications Office was set up in 1978, at the time when publishing for the British Library was hived off from British Museum Publications, who had handled it up until then. There is a total staff of eight, of whom five have mainly clerical duties, including order invoicing and credit control. A marketing officer was the first appointment after the Office had been set up by the Head of Publications, and it was in organising marketing – along with sales and distribution procedures – that the initial effort was made. A recently appointed publications editor makes up the complement of professional staff.

There is a backlist of about 175 titles, and about 15 titles a year are published. Turnover in 1982 was £350,000, and the annual budget (including salaries) runs at about £300,000. The policy is to run as a mixed economy; as well as its own publications (which include microfiches, posters, postcards as well as scholarly catalogues and some more general books), co-publishing is undertaken with many commercial and institutional publishers. A substantial income is forthcoming from royalties, mainly on the often large-scale programmes produced by microform publishers.

All design work is done by outside designers. The Office itself deals with all aspects of production, with the help of a freelance production consultant, and has never been involved with HMSO (the UK government printing office) – except on one occasion, when it acted as a commercial printer for the Library.

For the future, it is anticipated that the impact of new technology will lead to rationalisation in areas of the publishing programme which at present give some problems (for example, catalogues of oriental books). Given that many of the publications produced have only a limited market, potential improvements in printing techniques and costs for short-run books are being investigated keenly.

Deutsche Bibliothek, Frankfurt (Dr Gunther Pflug)

As the national library, the Deutsche Bibliothek adopts a comprehensive approach to acquiring German-language titles – and to this end some 200,000 books are bought annually. Arising from this policy, the Library's main publishing project is the *National Bibliography*, which runs to about 50,000 pages a year. The Library has its own phototypesetting equipment, and prepares the copy for the *National Bibliography*, but the printing, marketing and distribution are handled by commercial publishers. It thereby abides by the German government's regulations that lay down that no official institutions should be involved in activities that commercial agencies in a free market can do better.

In addition to the *National Bibliography*, exhibition catalogues (usually one or two a year) are produced, as are publications of standards and other information for librarians.

National Library of Scotland (Dr Ann Matheson)

The Library's publications officer is also publicity and exhibitions officer, with the result that such publishing as is done has been 'fitted in' according to the time and resources available to the officer. Over the last four years, the aim has been to expand the publishing programme, and in that period turnover has been raised from £400 to £12,000 annually.

The priority is given to publication of bibliographies, directories, catalogues of the Library's holdings, and union catalogues. Exhibition catalogues, commemorative publications and other projects aimed at a wider audience are also produced. Then there are 'moneyspinners', which tend to stress the 'Scottishness' of the Library – including postcards, T-shirts, erasers – which are sold both at a sales counter and by mail order.

The publications progamme is financed by money set aside from the Library grant; currently this is running at £50,000, to cover all Library publicity as well as publications.

Hugh Cobbe

Publishing policy

I was visiting a major research library a year or two ago during an investigation of other libraries' publication policies, and asked the administrator in charge of such things what their policy was. His answer was brief and to the point: 'We don't touch it if we can help it'! However, it emerged later on in our conversation that there were times when they couldn't help it.

I think that this is a position that all major research institutions find themselves in from time to time. There is, however, a great difference between being a re-active publisher and developing a publishing policy that is made to work. In the former case, the need to publish stems from a scenario such as this: Mr X donates to the Library a large and very valuable collection of, let us say, book-plates. One of the conditions of the donation is that a catalogue be produced and published, for which he may or may not be willing to pay. The desirability of the acquisition is balanced against the trouble and expense, in time and possibly money, of publishing the catalogue, and the former outweighs the latter. The local printer is consulted and it is decided, on his advice, to print 2,000 copies at an estimated cost of £3 each and it is planned to sell it at £3.50 – the extra cost to take account of postage. Because of lack of experience in preparing copy for the press on the part of the cataloguer, costs escalate and the copies are delivered together with a bill for £10,000, that is £5 a book. So the books are put on sale, at £5.50; and by the end of the first year 50 copies have been sold. The reaction from the administrators is, naturally enough, a cry of 'never again!'.

I happen to think that this scenario is not a typical one. On the other hand I do not think that any library would delude itself that it could, or should, compete with the major commercial publishers at their own game. Publishing, for many years an occupation for the dilettante, has in recent times become increasingly professionalised – to the extent that a career of marketing washing powders or motor cars can be a better training for a publisher than a lifetime spent with books. For it is a fact that to publish successfully, the production of books is only half the story; the establishment of criteria for performance of sales and the achievement of that performance is the other half. No library can hope to establish a selling machine that even palely imitates that of the successful commercial publisher and it would probably be extending itself beyond a judicious use of its resources if it tried to do so. Yet, given that publishing has become a professionalised industry with its own way of working and its own set of conventions, any publisher – in whatever context – is bound, if he is to meet with any success at all, to observe them insofar as they apply to what he is trying to do.

In approaching the problems presented by a publishing programme, the research library will not find itself applying the same criteria as the commercial publisher. By this I mean that the making of money will be only one of the objects to be achieved, for a library, being a depository of knowledge and information, has an obligation to those who use it (if it did not, there would be no point in its existence), and this cannot be expressed in simple commercial terms.

The nature of the user community will vary greatly from one library to another. The local branch of the County Library service will devote itself to serving its immediate neighbourhood; the main branch of the County Library will serve the interests of the county as a whole; the small college library will confine its priorities to serving the needs of the students in that college; the major university library will perceive a wider obligation to its own scholars and the community of scholars generally; the National Library will have the broadest obligation of all – not only to its own country but to the international world of libraries and book users, to the extent that in certain sectors it has a national representational, and thus, to put it very crudely, a propaganda function.

It is my view that, as the obligation to the user widens in scope beyond the immediate physical vicinity, so does publication come to play an increasing part as a means whereby the Library may fulfil this obligation, to an extent that publishing as an instrument of policy cannot be ignored by any library of more than local significance. It is by publication that a library can disseminate knowledge of its collections; it is by publication that a library can reproduce its holdings for the benefit of those who are unable physically to come to it (indeed, taking the concept of publication in the broadest sense, I would argue that the operation of a photographic service – a task which few libraries escape – is a form of publication, though we must leave that aside for the purposes of this seminar); finally it is by publication that the major world libraries support the library community, with the production of national bibliographies and the like.

This is not a new phenomenon. Certainly the British Museum and, more recently (since 1973) the British Library, have been publishing since the time of their respective foundations. The new phenomenon is the modernisation (if that is the best term) of the publishing industry, which has been constrained to conform in its practices to the aims and objectives of industry as a whole. Concepts formerly confined to more mundane manufacturing industries now apply in the same way to publishing; books have become 'product'. The challenge facing library publishing is the need to conform its practices to those of the publishing industry as a whole and yet, at the same time, to adapt the conventions of that industry so that those library objectives which cannot be described in purely commercial terms are not lost, but, if possible, even more surely achieved.

If the publishing industry has become professionalised, it is also true to say that the same has happened to librarianship. Library science and its twin, information science, are now a regular item on the curriculum in tertiary education. The library and publishing professions are, in a sense, complementary to each other but, curiously enough, do not overlap. Where the scope of the publisher ends, there begins the scope of the librarian. What we are examining here is a strange grey area where the two combine. It is not a large area; I am sure that library publishing will never be an especially significant sector of the publishing industry and I know that publishing is not one of the most pressing concerns of the library profession, but if library publishing is to be effective this area must be delineated and developed. Its inhabitants will need to have a foot in each camp and be equally at home in either.

How is this to be achieved? Let us first look at the case of a library that becomes involved in publishing for whatever reason but not to an extent that would justify setting up its own publishing unit; it will probably enlist the aid of a commercial publisher who will undertake to produce its books. A library with research collections does in any case find itself acting as a source for commercial publishers and this approach simply carries the process one stage further. The financial details of such arrangements can be complicated since the commercial partner will need to cover his overheads as well as the direct cost of producing the books. Partnerships of this kind are discussed later in this book (see pages 45–46). It is the simplest means of enlisting publishing expertise to the aid of the cause.

Larger libraries which have the resources to operate their own unit can – and I know five represented at this seminar have done this – meet the challenge by recruiting from the publishing industry. This is probably most effective if the publishing unit is large enough (ie more than one member of staff) for both librarians and publishers to be included. For publishers brought into the institutional environment will need, right from the start, to have the flexibility to adapt their expertise to the objectives of their employer, not all of which will necessarily be commercial and therefore familiar. Such people will often feel frustrated at the beginning, but even so I am sure it is easier for a publisher to turn librarian, at least to the extent required to be involved in an effective library publishing programme, than it is for a librarian to turn publisher. I speak as one who has attempted to do so. Many expert publishers come to grief in the maw of that elusive equation; the correct number of copies printed at the correct cost and sold at the correct price equals the successful publication. To one unversed in the ways of publishing this can prove a terrifying enigma!

Where circumstances warrant (and I think it is fair to say that this is likely to be very unusual in the library world) the extreme option is available of setting up a limited-liability publishing company, subject to all the rigours of company law and accounting rules. We shall be hearing about this in some detail later (see pages 9–13). All I would comment on this approach is that one needs to be very confident in one's market, before taking such a step. The more likely option in libraries will be to assign one or more officers to the task of handling a publications programme within the financial context of the institution as a whole. My thesis is that unless such officers have – or are ready to acquire – professional publishing expertise, a library publishing programme can all too easily fail to be effective.

I use the word 'effective' advisedly; the word that many an outsider would expect to be used in such a context is 'profitable'. I do not say that library publishing cannot be profitable, but I do say that profit is only one of the objectives that is likely to be sought in such a programme; it is as important that the programme should be a means of the library meeting its perceived obligations to its user community, as I said earlier, and we have seen that the larger the library the wider the community will be.

Participation in this seminar was limited, for practical reasons to representatives of major research libraries (with two exceptions) and so I wish briefly to consider the user communities that we may expect to encounter. First, there are of course the readers. They, perhaps, place the least demands on a publishing programme. They come to the library and they find what they want by means of in-house catalogues. However, as the significance of our holdings grows (I am thinking here not in a sense of time but in terms of a notional spectrum of libraries) so does the obligation to make them more widely available, in the first place to those to whom they are of the most immediate interest, whether it be a scholar in the humanities or in the sciences, whether we are talking about the academic or industrial world. In the largest libraries, matters go further, in that there comes an obligation to inform the general public particularly where, as in our own case, there is a high tourist 'visitorship', and, in a quite different direction, an obligation to support research work at the highest professional level in subjects of concern to the library community, such as library and information science and conservation and preservation.

For these members of the user community are legitimate objects for a publishing programme. It is the library publisher's task to define his various markets and use his expertise, not only to assess their extent, but also to ensure that the greatest possible market penetration is achieved. Any publisher needs to do this, but what makes it a particular challenge to the library publisher is that, without publishing expertise in his background, he will find it difficult to do, and even with it, he may find that he is attempting to do it with, as it were, one hand tied behind his back.

I say this, because one of the most fundamental differences that a publisher entering the institutional world will encounter is the matter of financial systems. I am sure that we would all agree that extreme flexibility and the potential for instant reaction to commercial opportunities are not notable features of most library finances. I am reasonably confident that most of us have had the experience of putting up a successful case for a new post in order to meet a clearly quantified increase in workload and, even so, having to wait for months or years before there is someone actually sitting in that chair. The bureaucratic procedures that appear to be inevitable in any institution of more than a certain size militate against the dynamic conduct of a publishing operation. This can extend even to the minutest areas, such as obtaining a new supply of pencils! In my experience, it is in this area that the greatest adjustment is required of someone entering the library world from publishing. I shall be especially interested to see if those who are here would agree.

Another major adjustment that will be required of the publisher entering the library world is an adjustment of his ideas of scale. In his previous career, he may well have been dealing with print-runs of tens of thousands; in his new one, he will find himself trying to see if he can print 150 copies of a specialist catalogue at a price that will make sense to the 150 people in the world who need to have that catalogue . . .

However, the publisher coming to the library environment will find there are enormous advantages too: a large library is staffed with potential authors; it is full of potential source material; he does not have to negotiate for the purchase of photographs and the right to publish them; it would be unusual for strictly commercial criteria which might dictate that a book is allowed a shelf-life of two years maximum before it is remaindered or pulped to be applied; on the contrary, the financial systems and policies of the institution, cumbrous though they may be, will probably allow him to take a broader view of cost recovery periods than his commercial counterpart and thus enable him to fund, or even subsidise, publications which – however desirable – would never in the ordinary way see the light of day.

This brings me to a point that I should like to make about perspectives that may arise in the library environment. A member of staff may spend up to ten years cataloguing an important collection of material. The cost to the library of all that time spent will run into tens of thousands of pounds – but it will have been decided that the collection justifies the investment. It is possible, therefore, to argue that the additional cost of publication is a minor consideration in comparison, regardless of the size of the market. This may be true, but it should also be possible to so publish the work and in such a quantity of copies that it still makes publishing sense.

Here technology is on our side. Printers are beginning to look seriously at means of production which can achieve an economic run of 100, or even 50, copies. There is also the increasing development of typesetting systems linked to word processors. A report sponsored by the British Department of Industry has recently castigated the publishing industry for its laggardliness in taking advantage of the opportunities offered by electronic typewriters and word processors: 82 per cent of publishers surveyed still used manual typewriters; 52 per cent had installed electric typewriters; 8 per cent had installed electric typewriters with word processing capabilities; 7 per cent had installed fully-fledged word processors – but only 3 per cent had linked these to typesetting systems. In contrast, the library community was quick to embrace the benefits of automated data processing and is thus in a much better position to take advantage of the technological developments by which ADP can be harnessed for the benefit of publications production. I hope that this is a topic which is raised in greater detail in the following papers and discussion. Suffice it to say here that the future for library publishing is considerably enhanced by new technology – at least we have found it to be so in the British Library.

I have said (several times) that the objectives of a library publishing programme will be to some extent non-commercial. Nonetheless, the final criteria for an effective programme must necessarily be financial. No budgets are unlimited and publishing expertise is required to ensure that they stretch as far as possible. An experienced publisher will produce ten books on a given budget, whereas a tyro will be lucky to produce half that number. A knowledge of book marketing techniques will ensure that the full sales potential of those ten books is realised, whereas a lack of it will ensure that many copies of those five books are still sitting in the warehouse five years later. However far an institution can afford to be less than strictly commercial, there can be little justification for producing publications that nobody wants. Probably many libraries will be well pleased if their publications programme pays for itself, for they are thus achieving part of their obligation to their users at no cost to themselves. However, to achieve this one must certainly aim higher and gear one's costs and charges to make a profit.

This raises the thorny question of profit on what? One can never achieve a clearly defined trading account when one is operating as part of a larger non-trading institution, because, in my experience, it is impossible to arrive at an equitable and agreed means of applying pro-rata shares of general costs. Indeed I am not entirely convinced of the worthwhileness of attempting to do so.

To sum up, therefore; as institutions we find ourselves with a need – if not always an inclination – to publish, to a greater or lesser degree. My point is that if we are to do this effectively we must do it professionally. I believe that the adaptation of the practices of the publishing industry to the needs of the library is one of the most exciting challenges facing our community of research libraries. We have been drawing to ourselves the raw material of knowledge, in a hundred years of expansion. The time is coming – indeed it has already come – when we must grasp every means to put such a resource to work for the benefit of society. Publishing is a means lying ready to hand, if it is used properly.

It is at this juncture that it makes sense for a seminar of this sort to take place, if for no other reason than to exchange information, at however basic a level. The British Library has taken the necessary steps to provide the forum, but it certainly has no wish to dominate the proceedings. My hope is that by pooling our common experience we shall leave the seminar better informed and perhaps even with a new perspective of the future.

Michael Hoare

Operating a publishing company

To appreciate the situation that British Museum Publications is in today it is necessary to look back to the past, to a time when a Keeper at the Museum would ask for money for a book and twenty years later a manuscript would emerge; when a printer would be summoned and, perhaps ten years after that, a book would actually be ready to be printed; when the printer asked the Keeper how many copies he should print, he would be told to print enough to last for ever; the book would then be published, lots of copies would be given away, and lots would be left. It is a measure of the success of this policy that in 1973, when the newly-established British Museum Publications inherited the old Museum stock, that stock included copies of the first edition of a book published in 1893, and still in print. At this point, the Trustees of the Museum said 'you are sitting on a goldmine' (a goldmine, however, with no working capital). So British Museum Publications came into being, and the experience may well be relevant to other institutions considering doing the same thing.

The real drawback to the old 'system' was the fact that it was almost impossible for the Museum to employ people with professional experience or qualifications in publishing. At the same time, the number of staff involved was part of the Museum's total headcount, and was therefore very tightly controlled. Bottlenecks inevitably occurred. The first advantage provided by setting up an independent publishing operation was the opportunity to employ qualified staff in the right quantity. As a corollary, a professional view of publishing possibilities and needs could be taken; the disciplines of cost control and a realistic view of the marketplace could be brought into play. Of course, it is very common for academics in museums – and libraries – to have an unrealistic view of the size of the market for a book, often finding it difficult to distinguish between academic 'importance' and the number of people who will actually buy the book, and so it is perhaps unsurprising that one reaction from Museum staff when BMP was established was horror ('a price being put on knowledge'). But of course profit in institutional publishing is not just financial profit. The fact is that BMP is in the fortunate position of publishing for 3 to 4 million visitors a year, most of whom are not academics and who certainly deserve a large amount of consideration, not just in terms of making a claim on their spending money but also in terms of serving their needs at their own level. BMP's ability to do this successfully means that the company is enabled to go on publishing the academic books, without looking for real 'profit', not attempting when pricing them to do anything other than to ensure that over ten years they 'recover their costs'. I hope that we have proved that to set up an independent publishing company in an institutional context does not mean that the books become more expensive.

There is a built-in opportunity and a built-in financial discipline in creating an independent publishing operation. It means that the company is not subject to the operation (with its pros and well as its cons) of government accounting; a surplus one year will not disappear the next year; on the other hand, there is no rolling fund appearing every year on which to fall back. Working a publishing programme into an essentially arbitrary financial programme can be very difficult and very frustrating.

Whatever the financial constraints, the key element in BMP's experience over the past ten years has been the proof that there is no substitute for a professional approach. This is not dependent on scale; even the smallest publishing operation can achieve it. Publishing does require specialist expertise, but it doesn't require an enormous amount of money to obtain that expertise. And it should extend to everyone involved in the operation; editors who know about editing more than they know about the subjects of the books they work on, marketing people who are able to identify and reach the potential purchaser of every book that is produced, and a publisher who is able to function effectively as the conductor of the orchestra rather than as any one of the musicians.

To have set up a company such as BMP during the past two years, when publishing has been so badly hit by the recession, would have been extremely difficult, and the extent to which government-funded operations have been able to continue without being so badly affected in that period would suggest that it wouldn't have been a very sensible move. Equally the extent to which it is considered desirable by institutions to hide their costs in order to get something published is bound to vary from place to place and from year to year. In the future, the option of hiving off the publishing operation could often be one that makes sense.

To finish, a quotation from Tennyson which expresses the culture-shock commonly experienced by a professional publisher encountering an institutional working environment for the first time:

And none can read the text, not even I:
And none can read the comment but myself.

Discussion

DANA PRATT: What is the position on taxability?

MICHAEL HOARE: The company has charitable status, and pays no corporation tax, because profits can be used only by the Museum. It is an extension of the Trustees' status. In setting up the company, there was a legal argument as to whether everything it produced had to be both charitable and educational. In the end an escape route was pointed out: to set up a wholly-owned subsidiary that is not charitable, which passes on all its income to the charitable company. This trading company therefore never makes a profit, so has to pay no tax.

DR GERAINT GRYFFYD: Do academic books still get published which you, as publisher, wouldn't in fact want to take on?

M.H.: As far as BMP is concerned, if the Trustees say that a book should be published, then it is – provided that not too many books come at once. It would be wrong for an institution's publishing company to be in a position to decide what the institution should be publishing; it can inspire publishing, but otherwise, in BMP's case, the Trustees' word is law.

G.G.: Does the Museum have a publishing committee?

M.H.: The Trustees' scholarship committee is very active. When a member of staff wants to publish, he or she fills in a form, on the basis of which BMP ask awkward questions (eg the estimated size of the market). Once approved, the publication is then in the pipeline. The most difficult thing then is to budget for when the copy is expected to be ready (more than one book has been promised for 'next year' every year that BMP has been in existence). A rule is imposed by BMP that nothing is spent on production until everything (complete copy, including bibliographies etc and all illustrations) is available.

G.G.: Do you obtain readers' reports?

M.H.: No. It is assumed that members of the Museum staff know what they are talking about.

HUGH COBBE: Would the BMP operation be viable without the Museum's 4 million annual visitors?

M.H.: No. Only on a very reduced scale.

H.C.: Should the lesson therefore be that one would have to think very hard about setting up a similar company, without such a flood of visitors?

M.H.: It rather depends on what other underwriting is available, over and above the number of visitors.

CHARLES ELLIS: I should like to give a gloss on what has been said, based on the experience of Library Association Publishing (like BMP, a limited-liability company), and thinking of the context of library publishing specifically. First, the notion of budgeting is totally different in libraries and other institutions from commercial operations: the 'budget' is what you are given each year, and beyond which you must not go. So when, for example, it comes to justifying the need for a new member of staff, this is always likely to be a long battle, and has to be planned for far in advance. Secondly, in a situation where a surplus is definitely required, this is generally achieved by keeping costs and overheads down. It is very often better to use outside people wherever possible, retaining only a core staff. 'Keep people off the payroll' is a motto that saves money. Thirdly, one must recognise that the concept of being 'self-financing' is a nonsense. Most commercial publishers are barely 'self-financing'. To be 'self-financing' at all you have to be going all-out to make a profit. You therefore need a committee of some sort spelling out from early on what this means, because otherwise projects get imposed upon the publishing unit which inhibit profit. Unfortunately this is a message which is rarely 'received' by the parent institution.

Robert Cross

Operating a publishing department

Publishing, whatever else it is, is first and foremost a business. If one keeps remembering this, it stops one from falling into that particular chasm which anyone who has worked in institutions such as ours knows all about. If your publishing unit is a separate body from its parent institution, it can of course be seen to jeopardise as well as enhance the activities of other parts of the institution; if it is an integral part, then the difficulty comes in persuading your lords and masters that what you are doing is investing, rather than expending, their money.

The basic rule is that a publishing department is investing money with the object of getting some return. Now of course it is very difficult in an institution to have the sole objective that the commercial publisher will have – of getting a profitable return. We are providing a service, after all. But it is a serious matter if we are not providing a return as well as that service; we have to sell our books, to get money coming back in, in order to reinvest in future projects, and also to determine the level of budget that we can hope to expect in future years. The problem is that this basic rule is all too easily forgotten. We can get very absorbed in the day-to-day business; and, in a scientific institution at least, we can become involved in grand bartering systems – one publication in exchange for another, or on the promise of another (the book you want promised, the one you don't want delivered first), and all paid for out of the publications budget.

The need to inform – indeed the perceived duty to inform – which for 99 per cent of the people in the institution is the service for which they are employed – induces a continuous fuzzing of the premise that the publishing department should be run as a business activity. And this brings one back to the essential need for professionalism within the publishing department. Publishing, as has been stated more than once in this seminar, is a specialised activity requiring people with the right training and experience.

To run an effective publishing department you must have a professional 'list-builder', someone whose job it is to plan for the long term, to direct and coordinate the publishing activities of the department. It is vital that this person has the ability and character to achieve a *modus operandi* with everyone within the institution. The list-builder should operate a system whereby any member of staff who purports to be a prospective author is required to fill in a forecast sheet every 6 months or so, giving an idea of what publications are in prospect; it is a good idea if these sheets are signed by the heads of departments, as a reminder of the obligations to which their members of staff are committing themselves. The system gives at least a rough idea of what is in the pipeline; some planning at least can be done, and the publishing department is not simply having to react to whatever happens to come its way. The system also serves to formalise what should essentially be an informal activity – the list-builder's role of listening to what prospective authors are doing in their research work (we should remember that the life of a researcher is often a lonely one), encouraging, with a view to shaping the best possible publication which can be achieved.

This leads me on to the production of publications. At the earliest stage there should be discussion with the author about the appearance of the publication, its extent, as well as the approach that the author is adopting. Traditional methods of production are becoming ever more expensive, and if you are able to get the author thinking in terms of microfiche, for instance, so much the better; the key thing is that they are not then disappointed that that is the way the publication appears. They have been involved in the decision to do it that way. And the publishing department can have the flexibility it needs in balancing up its output of books relative to publications in other media – and the choice of producing 25 microfiche publications, say, rather than 12 bound books that year, at the same total cost.

Once the publication is in production it is essential that a tight grip is maintained on the production schedule; this is true of course for any publisher, but even more is it true for the institutional publisher who is working to a yearly cash budget. If part of the production goes late, then it can literally happen that there is no money in the next year for the work to be done; or, more usually, it is the cause of another title being either re-thought or considerably delayed.

If there are large sums invested in publishing, then large amounts of money must come in as well. This is where the marketing of the publications is crucial. All the mailing lists are there – or at least they should be – but they must be coordinated in a professional marketing framework. We all should be able to be accurate about our markets; we should also have the means and the ideas to reach them.

I shall end by mentioning three other areas where it is essential for professional skill to be deployed. First, co-publications. There are often many opportunities for co-publishing arrangements, and these opportunities are worth working for; in most of our cases, it is probably true that the most worthwhile arrangement is one in which the institution does the publishing and runs on copies for another publisher (thereby keeping the control, and of course getting a useful cheque – which every publishing department should ensure can be used as a subsidy on its own publications). Secondly, debtor control. It is vital to have systems which enable you to keep a close watch on the flow of your income; no book is sold until you have the cash with which it has been bought. Thirdly, distribution. An efficient warehousing operation, tight inventory control, and the ability to supply books promptly are all vital, often unsung and overlooked, contributors to a successful publishing department. There is little point in producing good books and enticing people to buy them if you are unable to supply them within a reasonable time, or if you are yourself unable to say what stocks you hold at any particular time.

Discussion

HUGH COBBE: I should like to raise the issue of 'exchange' books. Would you agree that unless there is a paper transaction showing that the exchange department has actually 'bought' the books all hope of their being a true measure of the department's profitability is lost?

ROBERT CROSS: I quite agree; every transaction, internal as well as external, should be recorded and the cost covered in some way. Those who set the department's budget must face up to the costs that are involved, even where they are 'hidden'.

Q.: Can I ask Mr Hoare and Mr Cross what their policies are as regards price increases on backlist titles.

ROBERT CROSS AND MICHAEL HOARE: Prices are looked at every year, and while they have been edging up, it has not been in line with inflation. A publisher has to raise his prices sometimes. The exciting thing, however, is that sales usually go up as a result: booksellers are more prepared to stock a book, the more expensive it becomes and the higher their own cut is.

DANA PRATT: On the question of those 'mouldering manuscripts' it may be of interest that the Library of Congress has instituted a similar rule to that imposed by Michael Hoare and Robert Cross in their respective institutions. Nothing is done until the complete manuscript is in hand. On the question of budgeting, it has always seemed curious to have money coming in and going out, but no direct connection between them; but it does seem to be something that most of us here have to put up with.

ALEC BOLTON: What are other people's policies as regards payments of royalties to members of staff?

M.H.: BMP have a series of books, called Colonnade Books, on which a royalty is payable. These are more general books, commissioned on a commercial basis, carried out in members of staff's own time. Authors of official publications, done in Museum time, do not get a royalty.

A.B.: Does this affect your pricing?

M.H.: Yes, it does. But then the more popular books are likely to have longer print-runs, so it tends to even out.

NICOLAS BARKER: Everyone so far has seemed to be describing that phenomenon of the past fifteen years, by which institutional publishing has been becoming 'professional'. In a library context, trade and academic publishing has changed too. Does this new approach mean that a new type of publishing is emerging?

M.H.: In many ways it is an old kind of publishing that is re-emerging – it is akin to the old concept of a university press.

HUGH COBBE: One could say, though, that our type of publishing is more conducive to modern techniques, particularly techniques of production and of production in many media. There are great opportunities to be taken in this area.

John Mitchell

Production techniques for short-run reference books

If the microfiche is the pantechnicon of reference for the librarian the book is his hand tool, the wicker basket. Like any other tool which has been in use for a long period it has acquired a patina, a familiar feel and a design which, because it is functional, is also attractive.

The requirements of books which are to be used primarily as tools can be summarised:

— They should be compiled and typographically designed for ease of reference.
— They should be able to stand up to use over a long period.
— Their cost should be economic.

There are two factors which fundamentally affect economy of production. First, the information may be lengthy, typographically complex and may include passages in foreign, sometimes oriental, languages. Secondly, the number of copies which will meet the needs of this specialised readership may be measured in hundreds of copies rather than the thousands which make commercial publishing viable. Preparation of the information up to the point that it is in a state fit for printing is the most time-consuming and expensive part of the operation for the author and the printer. Typesetting costs can reach 70 per cent or more of the total cost of production. It is in this area that new technology is being applied to reduce cost and at the same time allow an acceptable method of presenting the material. The conjunction of photography and computer technology has opened up completely new means of preparing copy for the press and for printing it.

At the most basic level, the author's handwriting can be reproduced, which can be effective with some of the exotic scripts. At the next level, the author's typewritten text can be reproduced. A development from this is the use of the word-processor, with which the author can create a file which is directly readable by a computer-controlled typesetting machine. Finally, there is photo-typesetting, carried out under the control of a skilled operator.

In real terms photo-typesetting is both cheaper and a great deal more flexible than the hot-metal system which preceded it. It is easy to mix sizes and styles of type: it is possible to create special characters at reasonable cost. The product can, with thoughtful typographic design and cooperation from the author, provide the clearest and most effective means of conveying information. But, because it involves the use of complex machinery and expert manipulation, it is the most expensive method of creating a printable image. So it is primarily for reasons of economy that the other methods have come into use.' And they can be effective if the different limitations which each impose can be accepted.

The reproduction of typewritten material has become accepted in some types of work. The most obvious limitation is in the inflexible nature of the machine: even with the use of a variety of golfballs or daisy-wheels the size of type and the variety of accents and special characters is severely limited. The design of the type is also restricted and tends to look anaemic on the printed page. Photographic reduction improves its appearance but it is usually less economical of space than conventional type. The clear advantage is that the cost of typesetting is eliminated: the author becomes his own typesetter. But in addition to editorial accuracy, this places upon him the discipline of consistency of style and of design of the page – matters which he would otherwise expect to be dealt with by the publisher and printers.

The word-processor offers a wider range of functions and, in particular, storage capacity, from which a file can be created which will activate a typesetting machine. On the face of it, this seems to offer the best of both worlds. The cost of typesetting can be reduced by more than half – but the discipline imposed on the author is even greater. Not only has he to have all his words and points of style correct, but he has also to introduce coding into the typescript, in order to instruct the typesetter's computer as to the size and style of type. The compositor does no more than convert the author's command codes to those which the machine will accept. Just how far authors – or their typists – are prepared to go in the direction of being a typesetting operator has yet to be established. It is also somewhat debatable whether or not the method is cost-effective. It is likely that it can be so for simple work: for example, where there is seldom need to change the type style and where there are few diacriticals or other requirements which call for individual coding.

Whatever the means, the typographic design of the page is important. It can, and should, enhance the author's intentions, and at its best can greatly aid ease of reference and the utility of the book.

Printing is almost certain to be by the photo-lithography process. Letterpress is no longer appropriate for this type of work and photocopying has limitations in the size of paper which can be used. The advantages of photo-litho printing are that it will accept a wide range of qualities and substances of paper; that illustrations can readily be incorporated; and that the larger machines will print a sheet size large enough to be folded and allow of section sewing. The most common complaint of the process is that the printing is grey by comparison with letterpress, which can be a valid cause for concern, and is often apparent on books reproduced from typewritten material.

At the present state of the art, photocopying, although producing a strong clear image, is restricted in the size of paper which can be used and in the qualities which it will accept.

The printing itself is the least costly element of production and is commonly closely matched by the cost of the paper. Bearing in mind the longevity which is frequently expected of books of this nature, the choice of paper is important. The selection, however, is often limited to the range carried in stock by paper merchants, because the quantity needed for one title is insufficient to justify it being made to a particular specification. Most book papers are made from chemically bleached wood pulp with some additives. This is a naturally short-fibred and fairly weak type of paper and it can discolour and become brittle with age. The last two faults can be minimised by specifying that it should be acid-free. The inherent weakness can be overcome by using a reasonably heavy weight, which also has the advantage of ensuring good opacity. The range of shades in stock papers is also limited, but in general a slightly cream tone is preferable to a hard white for readability.

Equally important for longevity and for the type of use which is to be expected for reference books is the binding. This is an aspect of book production which has not been dramatically affected by modern technology; the sequence of events in a mechanised bindery is much the same as can be seen in a hand bindery and, superficially at least, the end product looks similar. Books which have been printed on sheet sizes allowing 16 pages or more in sections can be folded and section-sewn before being lined and cased in cloth-covered boards. Modern adhesives are more flexible than animal glues and so aid opening the book without breaking its back. There are variations in binding technique which can offer economies, of which unsewn (or 'perfect') binding is the most common. Originally designed for cheap paperback production, the backs of the sections in this process are sawn off and adhesive forced into the fibres of the paper. The glue is thus the principal factor in the strength of the binding, although it is reinforced with a lining. The method is slightly cheaper than sewing and is the only method that can be used to case-bind books produced by photocopying or printed on small photo-litho machines.

In reference books the jacket is usually as functional as the book it protects: a simple typographic exercise on strong paper, to keep the book clean between the end of its production and the beginning of its life on the library shelf. Shrink-wrapping has the same effect at less cost, though it is necessary to be careful that the books are not wrapped before they are dry from the binding operations. Moisture in the adhesives tends to be absorbed by the paper and can cause cockling. This will normally dry out, but is initially unsightly – and is especially unwelcome in a volume which, however economically produced, is likely to be expensive.

For as long as librarians look to books as a prime source of reference there will be room for well-produced and thoughtfully designed printing and binding. There will still be a place for the wicker basket beside the driver of the pantechnicon.

Discussion

HUGH COBBE: It is interesting that a number of printers are looking at the possibilities of economic short-run production facilities, aiming at the same time to maintain a high standard of production. For example the British Library had been able to make its *Bibliography of Estonian Books* a viable proposition when at first it had not seemed to be one. It is important that the camera-ready copy that is prepared is as good as it is possible to make it.

DANA PRATT: The Library of Congress had sent the copy of its catalogue of the Vietnamese holdings in the Library to a Hong Kong setter. Unfortunately none of the errors were 'corrected'. The moral is that setters only set the copy they are given.

MICHAEL HOARE: It is important to be aware of the limitations of typewritten camera-ready copy. First, with the likely amount of typewriting capacity that there will be on call, it is difficult to do anything in a hurry; one or two books at a time will probably be the maximum. Secondly, there is the problem of editorial overload. The editor has to design the book as he goes along; and while there may not be any proofs to correct, it is still a very time-consuming process.

Alec Bolton

Marketing (1)

I went to the National Library of Australia in 1974 from an editorial background in commercial publishing in Sydney and London. Differences of attitude between commercial and library publishing struck me as very great. In my experience, the commercial publisher had been very sensitive to the reaction of important bookseller customers, and constantly obtained feedback through his sales representatives on how his books were being received. By contrast, the library publishing office seemed remote from its customers. Those customers tended to be the acquisition departments of other libraries, rather than known individuals. Dealings were more impersonal and were conducted mainly through the mail. Ordering procedures were slow. Orders did not always seem to express an actual wish to have something. There was a sense of being isolated from the end user.

It must also be said that marketing considerations did not always play a large part in determining what the Library would publish. Many publications were issued in fulfilment of statutory obligations under the National Library Act, and others were reflections of institutional policy developments. Much of the total publishing activity was justified on grounds other than those of sales potential. In the operation as a whole, successful marketing was not crucial to survival, and this seemed to me to be the main difference between the commercial and the library field.

Today the situation has changed to some extent, and publishing activities have become more market-orientated and, I believe, more realistic. Government policies in the past ten years have asserted the need for cost-recovery, and this has led to significant changes in attitude. In the past, many publications were only nominally priced, and there was a large free distribution. Today, prices reflect actual costs of production, and the free distribution of publications within Australia has virtually ceased. Australian libraries have been educated to pay for publications of the National Library.

These changes have coincided with years of economic recession in which the budgets of Australian libraries have contracted in real terms. Libraries have become more selective and discriminating in their acquisitions, and this has had implications for the National Library as a publisher. We used to think, for example, that the demand for our most important serial publication, *Australian National Bibliography,* would be relatively inelastic. This was not correct. In our quest for cost recovery, the price of subscription to the full service of the *National Bibliography* increased by over 700 per cent between 1972 and 1982 – more than four times the inflation in the same period. Many subscribers fell away, or enrolled for cheaper services. By the end of 1982 we were modifying the format and reducing the typesize in order to contain the size of the publication and to hold the price from rising further. At the same time we were questioning whether the *National Bibliography* had a viable future as a printed publication.

Changes like these have challenged complacency and made us more responsive to the market. Attitudes to customers are more positive and there is greater anxiety to give efficient service. At the same time, there is an increasing awareness on our part of the growing revenue objectives that are laid upon the Publications Branch of the Library, the attainment of which affects the availability of funds for other National Library purposes, including acquisitions.

Traditionally, we engage in two types of marketing – to libraries and to bookshops. Our bibliographical and our service publications – dealing with various aspects of library science – are sold direct to other libraries by subscription and mail order. Possibly 10 per cent of the business is done through subscription agents and library suppliers. We give them 10 per cent discount on subscriptions and 25 per cent on monograph orders. But 90 per cent of the business is done direct at the full price, through the mail. The price we set on this kind of service material is always inclusive of postage.

Our main customers in this field are drawn from a group of about 1,600 libraries to which we regularly send announcements. For important publications we sometimes print a run-on of the cover on a lightweight art paper, with a blurb and order form on the back. Librarians may not judge a book by its cover, but it helps sales to give them an idea of what it is like.

For publications in series and those that appear annually, we try to persuade customers to place standing orders. An annual list of publications in print is issued to all customers and is made liberally available.

From time to time we do a wider promotion to libraries by purchasing a commercial mailing list. Respondents are added to our own list. We have used the library lists of IBIS Information Services to mail material about National Library publications and services to upward of 5,000 libraries in Australia, including 2,400 secondary schools. However, the last time we did this – about 12 months ago – we attracted only about 200 new customers.

Australia is a large country with a small, dispersed population. It is not possible to visit libraries to show new publications to them. One way of compensating for this is to take space for displays at trade fairs and conferences which libraries are attending. The best of these, for us, is the two-yearly conference of the Library Association of Australia, at which up to 1,500 librarians may be present, out of a total Australian membership of 7,500. But smaller meetings of specialists – for example, of map specialists, or of librarians dealing with services to the handicapped – can be well worth while for exhibiting publications in a particular subject area. We have used National Library delegates to such meetings to promote sales. The subject expert is often the best sales person for a specialised work.

Our marketing to bookshops involves a small output of trade publications – two or three a year – intended for general sale as well as library sale. They are a minor part of our activity but they generate about one-third of our revenue.

We use a commercial distributor for the books in this programme. We retain responsibility for review copies and advertising. The distributor carries our stock on consignment and handles representation to booksellers, distribution and account collection. It is very costly. We give booksellers 40 per cent discount, and the distributor's commission is 27.5 per cent of the invoice value. The net return is thus only 43 per cent of the retail price. Unless we can set a high retail price, we have to sell a very large proportion of the edition to break even. We do not have to pay royalties out of our return of sales; fees in lieu of royalties are added in as a component of production costs.

Marketing a small list of a scholarly or semi-scholarly nature is not easy. Frankly, we find it unsatisfactory to rely on a distributor, but it is necessary to have someone to show new books to the trade, and to pursue repeat orders, and the cost of doing this ourselves would be prohibitive, with such distances to cover. In any event, the level of bookshop interest is disappointingly low.

More and more we see sense in trying to sell direct to the final customer, particularly if a book has a defined audience. We think it is worth investing time and money to build a special mailing list for the individual title, using the contacts of the author or editor as a starting point.

Last year we published a book of wildflower paintings derived from one of our special collections. It was a 1,500-copy printing and a $78 book. Starting from a published list of societies and associations, we built up at little cost a mailing list of nearly 15,000 people known to be interested in botany and in Australian art, and in such things as bushwalking, conservation, the cultivation of native plants and so on. We did a lavish brochure and made a pre-publication offer of $55 to these people. The response was about 4 per cent, so that on publication day we had sold 600 copies or 40 per cent of the edition, and had covered over 90 per cent of the total expenditure on the book and the promotion. We don't regard this experience as especially brilliant, but we believe it was an indicator of the way we should go in the future.

The other form of direct selling that is very valuable is the co-edition. Finding an overseas publisher to take part of the printing under a separate imprint is very time-consuming, and it can mean a long postponement of publication. But it lowers the unit cost while at the same time generating revenue. Our one recent experience of selling two co-editions of a National Library publication turned what would have been a financial failure into a small success.

I would like to conclude by saying that in the publishing office of our library we tend to be preoccupied with editorial and production problems. There is always a danger of forgetting that it is harder to sell publications than it is to produce them. I am hoping to lift our marketing performance through the shared experience of this seminar.

Jane Carr

Marketing (2)

An essential difficulty for everyone involved in publishing in libraries or governmental institutions is that the disciplines of the market-place are largely unknown, even alien, to the majority of one's colleagues, whether they be librarians, scholars or administrators. The need at least to recover direct costs in a publishing venture requires that the market be determined not by what people *should* want but by what they are already known to want or can be persuaded so to do. In this situation 'marketing' may challenge the 'intrinsic worth' argument for publication, and that challenge requires justification or, at least, explanation.

In pursuit of a definition for marketing in the library publishing context I spent a thoroughly enjoyable – but, as it turned out, entirely wasted – Saturday afternoon in the Reading Room of the British Library. For the view that marketing is all-embracing, I found David Carson, an American and author of *International Marketing: a comparative systems approach*. In his view, 'the integrated marketing concept has been pushed to the point where the head of marketing becomes the chief executive officer'. An attractive idea, but not one likely to attract much support. Besides, advocates for the opposing school – that marketing, like history is bunk – were too numerous to be ignored. I wandered from Marx and Mill to the current American schools and became more and more convinced that the most general usage of the term is to add status and respectability to the more vulgar term 'sales'.

I turned back to my own experience. In the context of library publishing the term 'marketing' is used most consistently in a negative sense – to describe the absence of activity rather than its presence. Thus, if a new title fails to attract the sales expected of it, or if an existing publication is suffering from declining sales, the failure is likely to be attributed to a lack of marketing expertise (meaning 'we don't know what went wrong'). If a title succeeds, 'marketing' is unlikely to be cited as a reason for success. Instead the quality of production, or the effectiveness of promotion, or even the efficiency of distribution, will be the reasons discussed.

Is this not an answer in itself? For marketing to be successful – and therefore self-justifying – we must analyse its constituent parts and decide at the outset what is expected from any 'marketing' initiative. The term means nothing without the analysis.

Common sense and experience allow for broad divisions: to define, or even create, a market for a particular product or group of products; to establish how best that market can be reached and what price (if any) it will bear; and to ensure that the product reaches the market. In the specific context of our own publishing I interpret the marketing role in the publishing process as

— to advise on the likely size of market for a book and to participate in the decisions on print-runs (even to question the decision to publish at all)

— to advise on a suitable price, taking into consideration not only the cost of production but also the optimum market price

— to make suggestions on the physical appearance of the book and its suitability for the market envisaged

— to establish the best method of promoting that book (whether by direct mail, review copies, advertising, bookshop visiting)

— to ensure efficient accounting and distribution.

Within that definition, there seem to be three key areas to which library publishing tends to give insufficient attention. First, pricing and print-runs. Too often the conflicting demands for a low retail price and low unit cost lead to decisions to publish too many copies at too low a price, leaving a warehouse or stockroom embarrassingly full of unsold copies and equally embarrassing failure to achieve recovery even of printing costs. Sometimes the print-run is arrived at without consideration of the size of the potential market at all, or else stems from undue optimism or circumspection (a failure by no means exclusive to library publishing).

Secondly, accounting and distribution. Efficient invoicing and despatch are vital for the smooth running of a publications office, however small. Nothing is more embarrassing (or more likely to prejudice future sales) than a customer's complaint of 'snail-like service', duplicated supply or incomplete information on an invoice. (In the past we have been accused of all three and many more; and more time has been wasted in our office unravelling our own mistakes and inefficiencies in this area than in anything else). Equally, the internal combination of budgetary restraints and pressure to increase revenue require organised

Marketing (2)

accounting. Credit control, for example, is vital if you decide to supply on credit as well as by pre-payment. And here it is worth mentioning that the effect of efficiency in this area is to improve morale and to encourage a positive approach in staff who might otherwise feel their only purpose is to keep the auditors happy. As a further important by-product of efficient accounting, it should also be possible to produce sales records and reports which will allow detailed evaluation of past performance and accurate prediction of the potential market for future projects.

For warehousing and distribution, an option – which is ours at present – is to use a commercial operation. We know that stock is secure, that it is stored efficiently and at the right temperature and that books are despatched within 24 hours of receipt of an invoice. Overseas orders are well packed and have the correct documentation, and inland orders are supplied by carrier as well as by post. The real cost of farming out distribution may mean that it is an option that cannot even be considered; but, however it is to be achieved, efficient warehousing and distribution should be a prime consideration – if only to allow resources to be concentrated on the key creative processes of selecting and producing the books themselves.

Thirdly, mailing lists. Whether we sell direct or through library suppliers, the bulk of our sales are (and will continue to be) the library and institutional markets. Direct mail must, therefore, be the main method of approach, and the success of direct mail promotion depends not only on the production of appropriate mailing pieces but, vitally, on the quality of the lists themselves. Specialist lists can be bought from brokers and, in spite of the high cost, this can be the most sensible option – as long as care is taken over selection. But, if resources allow, I would strongly advocate the maintenance of internally-held lists, at least for the core library market. Given that most of the information required for the maintenance and up-dating lists can be found within our own libraries, results should more than justify the effort.

Our own experience has proved this on a number of occasions and we are now about to transfer our manual lists onto a microcomputer, using a simple package which virtually replicates a card index but which includes codes to allow searches by subject, institutional type or geographical area. (Introducing the system has been an eye-opener – fascination with the new technology has brought forth for our use a number of newsletter and specialist lists already held in the Reference Division.)

Catalogues and leaflets: like many others, we produce an annual complete list of our publications, and a series of leaflets or fliers on individual titles or groups of titles. The first and only lessons are obvious – that copy and production should be suited to the market for which they are intended. Leaflets on individual titles are not always necessary, and there is no point in producing mailing pieces if you have not already decided on a mailing programme.

For advertising (and by this I mean buying space in national or specialised newspapers and journals and even local radio) I can only express a personal view – and that is that advertising is rarely effective unless you have a large enough budget to make a real and sustained impression. With a small budget there are usually – though not always – better ways of producing results.

In the library context review coverage is one of these. Maintaining review lists for specialist journals is essential, and personal contacts with editors or literary editors is always worthwhile. Statistics vary on librarians' response to reviews as a source of information, but they are generally second or third after listings in national bibliographies and specialist leaflets.

Finally I will mention two aspects of selling to booksellers and library suppliers, with the qualification that they only apply to those whose list has genuine trade potential.

First, discounts. With a background in general publishing, it may be that I have a greater inclination to support the bookseller or library supplier than others involved in library publishing. Nevertheless, I would maintain that to sell to bookshops, and to persuade them to stock our titles and thus to provide exposure to the general reader which we cannot hope to achieve ourselves, we must accept normal trade practices and budget for them. We have opted for a sliding scale – 35 per cent on general titles, 25 per cent on bibliographies and reference works, and 10 per cent for microfiche publications and serial subscriptions. Bookselling margins are small and reasonable discounts are essential. Returning to the Reading Room, I find historical support for this view. In a letter to the Clarendon Printing House, Dr Johnson advocates the need for more liberal discounts to induce booksellers 'to circulate academical publications'. Little has changed since the eighteenth century; he proposes that 'we must allow, for profit, between thirty and thirty-five per cent . . .'

A final word on representation – by which I mean the employment of representatives to present publications in person to booksellers and, possibly, to acquisitions librarians and academics. Even to consider representation requires substantial turnover, an organised publishing programme and a list which can genuinely profit from so costly a sales method.

We have hovered on the brink of taking this step for almost two years now, and still cannot be sure that it would be fully justified. In the UK, to employ one representative would cost in the region of £25,000 a year and is clearly out of the question. To employ freelance representatives on a commission of around 12.5 per cent is the only possible option and this requires not only considerable confidence in the prospect of much-improved sales, but also some degree of certainty that our titles will not come at the end of a long list from other publishers with greater potential than ours and, therefore, with greater earning capacity for the freelance.

It is worth adding here that representation in foreign markets may, surprisingly, be easier to achieve. The appointment of foreign agents to promote and sell our publications may prove time-consuming in the initial assessment and negotiation phases (it certainly was with our own efforts) but is worth considering in markets where substantial interest has been identified but where lack of direct experience prevents the conversion of that interest into worthwhile sales (a possible area for cooperation among publishers worldwide, if only for local advice?).

The one great advantage for library publishers is that the material available to them is likely to be unique – we even have our authors on the premises and can control the use of our library's resources. It is an advantage for which most publishers would give their right arm (or at least delegate the privilege to members of their staff). In combining the functions of providing access to information and resources and of producing revenue, there is every reason to exploit that advantage. And we should not forget that in doing so we are presenting an image not just of our publishing list but of the library itself.

Discussion

DR CLIVE FIELD: Is it actually worth sending out review copies? Do not the reviews come out too late?

JANE CARR: It is worth it, but only if you are selective.

NICOLAS BARKER: Reviews are the lifeline for this kind of publishing, as long as the publisher is efficient in organising them. What is more, reviews 'satisfy the author'.

MICHAEL HOARE: It is important to do some advertising, not least because it keeps the journals that review your books in business.

ALEC BOLTON: We budget for about 50 review copies per title, we attempt to alert literary editors to forthcoming books, send them advance copies etc. We have sometimes been successful in obtaining reviews in national newspapers. Late reviews can still be helpful, particularly for slower-selling titles, and they can be good for 'plugging' another edition of the book.

J.C.: One should not forget the possibility of trading the placing of an advertisement for some space in the editorial matter.

HUGH COBBE: There is of course the possibility of placing inserts and leaflets in journals. I am wondering if others have tried this, and if they have, whether they can answer the question – 'how can you tell if it has worked'?

M.H.: Getting one's money back fast can often be as important as getting it all back over a period of years. For this reason we have had some success with very expensive publications by introducing a special price for a period of six months or so. It hurries libraries up. But it has to be a decent saving on the final price.

J.C.: We did that for our microfiche *General Catalogue of Printed Books Supplement*. The special offer lasted only two months, and it was very successful, with some 250 orders coming in that period.

M.H.: Two months seems too short a period: six months seems fairer.

KEN CARPENTER: I should like to ask how one can ever determine a print-run or know what the market is for a book. 'Libraries will have to have it' – and they certainly don't like to say no, at least not when you ring them up and ask if they would buy a certain book – but in practice they don't always.

J.C.: You can go back to your previous experience for titles which are similar to others published in the past. Otherwise you can go and talk to publishers who have experience of similar titles. I agree that this is easier with reference works: general books are much trickier, and here the proverbial 'gut feeling' (which I define as 'instinct allied with common sense') is what has to be relied on.

H.C.: This is an absolutely crucial question. There is hardly any aspect of publishing more likely to induce nightmares. Getting the print-run (and thus one's assessment of the market) wrong so often means that a book, which may sell relatively well, ends up making no contribution to one's 'profit'.

K.C.: Determining the print-run is also vital, of course, when negotiating with a co-publisher.

ROBERT CROSS: During such negotiations it is vital to pin down the co-publisher on what his mark-up will be, and have a clause in the contract stating 'no price increase within 18 months of publication'.

A.B.: The most important marketing decision may often be, not to proceed with a title.

H.C.: It might be of interest to others to hear my own rule of thumb calculation for the different categories of books that we publish:
Very obscure catalogues (Slavonic, oriental etc) – 150–350 copies.
Fairly obscure bibliographies – 500 copies.
Catalogues of Manuscripts – 500 copies.
Less obscure catalogues – 750–1,000 copies.
General titles – minimum of 1,500–2,000 copies. (With 'blockbusters' up to 5,000 copies.)
Co-publication deals – 5,000–10,000 copies in total.

JOANNA DODSWORTH: The most difficult kind of publication to get right is the exhibition catalogue. It is nearly impossible to predict the number of visitors to an exhibition, and certainly impossible to say how many would actually buy the catalogue. Price is critical here, too.

H.C.: I certainly second that. One of my own nightmares was the catalogue we produced (in far too great a quantity) for an exhibition on 'Diplomacy'. Conversely, the catalogue we produced for an exhibition on 'The Benedictines in Britain' sold very well. Perhaps it depends on the potential market after and outside the exhibition itself; perhaps such catalogues should simply be thought of in the same way as other general books.

Heather Dean

Retailing in on-site bookshops

We are all, or most of us, very lucky; we must be the envy of every commercial publisher. We have captive audiences, and we can sell our publications on our own premises. A considerable part of our total market actually comes to us – both museums and libraries – every year. All libraries share this advantage and none can afford to ignore it.

The advantage cannot be disputed. Looking more closely, it can be broken down to the following:

— We should be able to provide a service to the public which they cannot get elsewhere.

— There is a great potential for 'impulse buys'.

— We shall be getting a greater return (selling at full retail price).

— The sales life of our books is lengthened.

— We can establish a 'publisher profile'.

— We can do special promotions for any of our titles.

This becomes particularly true as bookshops increasingly choose very carefully what books they stock, and for how long. For the hesitant buyer who may have read a review of a book, actually to see the book can have a decisive effect.

Setting up and running a shop need not be too complicated. For the smaller institutions it may simply be a display of titles at the information desk; for others, a separate kiosk will be required. Where there is permanent exhibition space, a full-scale shop will be desirable – and it can be argued that it improves the experience of the visit. Whatever the size of the operation, the same techniques apply.

In the British Museum's case, the shop is run by a professional bookshop manager. This I regard as vital; enthusiastic amateurs should not be encouraged. The manager's responsibilities can be broadly divided into three:

1. Staff selection. He or she will be looking for retail experience, and will tend to avoid the keen arts graduate (who is unlikely to stay keen for long). Training courses help, but otherwise it is a matter of briefings on selling techniques, and instilling product knowledge. It is essential that sales staff know how to handle money – and this includes, in our case, credit cards and traveller's cheques, as well as cash. Staff motivation is perhaps best gained by introducing a profit-sharing scheme.

2. Display. There are plenty of purpose-built display units available. New titles will be given prominence, all books will be shown face forward if at all possible, and will be stacked up in large piles. There should be awareness (on the part of all staff) of potential tie-ins to TV or special talks being given in the Museum, so that these books can be drawn attention to. The expensive scholarly monographs, while they may be behind glass, should also be available for handling.

3. Housekeeping. There is no point installing spotlights if the lightbulbs are never replaced. All stocks should be in mint condition.

Whatever the size of the sales point or status of the manager, attention to these points should serve to maximise turnover. The aim should be to make using the shop a habit for visitors.

The next step is to consider extending the retail function – buying in from other publishers, and merchandising. The important point to bear in mind is the market's need; is an ever-changing stock necessary? Are you mostly selling to children, or academics, or foreign visitors, or local residents? Certainly, if you decide to go down this road, you are likely to be able to mount a more attractive display – which will help the sales of your own books. But equally it will improve your own margins. It pays to encourage staff to suggest possible books to stock; at the same time, slow-sellers must be dropped, special discounts negotiated from publishers – and low-discount items not stocked at all.

As for merchandising (which you will be buying in from specialist manufacturers), the possibilities are very great; erasers, address books, calendars, tapestry kits, replicas, pens, badges – we stock all these and more. More realistically, nearly all publishing libraries will be producing posters and postcards. In our case, the British Library postcards are very good sellers (their advice, and mine, is to make them pretty, not 'academically important'); and why not put them to other uses – packaged on a theme, with accompanying notes, or employed as the cover of spiral notebooks? Some subjects make excellent jigsaws, too. Posters can present a storage (and display) problem; but, provided this can be overcome, and provided they are decorative enough, they can often be steady sellers. There are two distinct markets – the school visitor and the tourist – and you should aim to have posters for them (not everyone can have Magna Carta, which appeals to both).

What is the next step? A mail-order operation is an obvious extension of this type of business (the Metropolitan Museum in New York is the supreme example). It will promote your name, and encourage visitors. As long as you don't run out of stock of the catalogue, or mail it to the wrong addresses, it should also make you some money. But for the average institution, it is probably more sensible to think about getting in on other people's mail-order catalogues. In the UK, a cooperative museums mail-order scheme has been quite successful in promoting sales.

A well-run retail operation, then, can make a considerable contribution to the service that a library offers.

Discussion

JOANNA DODSWORTH: It has taken nearly three years to get plans through for a new Bodleian shop. It is perhaps just a part of the shock one feels when coming into an institutional environment – but it still seems a very long time for a comparatively simple change. We shall also be faced with the difficulty of not being able to recruit specialist staff.

MICHAEL HOARE: It is one of the chief advantages of being an independently run company that we are able to select all our staff – and can therefore employ sales assistants, rather than re-train warders.

HUGH COBBE: What is the 'bottom line' for setting up a shop?

M.H.: It will depend on your resources, the number of visitors – and your own priorities. You will have an initial fitting-up outlay (perhaps £5,000–£10,000). Then, depending on the discounts you achieve on bought-in stock, there should be a minimum 45 per cent gross margin. You should be able to extract money from any number of visitors; many don't feel they have 'visited' the place unless they carry something away with them. In our case, the shop is selling to roughly 20 per cent of the people who come to the Museum, and the average sale per person is 30p.

DR KARL DACHS: In our case, the proportion is 10 per cent of visitors.

STEPHEN GREEN: For libraries on multiple sites, it is often worth selling a limited range of postcards at the different sites; it is part of the service, and it helps fill in the time when waiting for books.

RACHAEL GOLDSTEIN: In Columbia's case, our visitors are largely academics, and we sell to them through the campus bookstore.

HEATHER DEAN: An opportunity for marketing your products as 'gifts that are different', perhaps?

JANE CARR: In such cases, it may well be worth giving the bookstore a special display case or encouraging a special promotion.

DR CLIVE FIELD: We used to sell postcards in the university bookshop; when we sold them in the library instead, we sold six times as many.

M.H.: When choosing staff, it is always worth remembering that often the people behind the counter are the only ones that visitors will ever speak to – and you want them to create a good impression.

DANA PRATT: For this reason, perhaps, in the Library of Congress the shop staff are paid for out of the Information Desk budget.

J.C.: To end on a warning note; one knows cases of bookshops being set up in libraries, and failing. The key to it is to start slowly, and build, rather than buy in a superb display and then find that you are not able to get the stock turnover you wanted.

Dana Pratt

Operating a publishing programme through outside agencies

My experiences with outside publishers, which may be applicable to others, suggest that the first advantage of operating a publishing programme through a commercial publisher or university press is one of scale; one is able to take advantage of their marketing leverage – far greater than that which one may have oneself. As a result, the books get into the bookstores. The second advantage is what I would term the 'OPM' factor; one is using 'other people's money'. So, if you can get a publisher interested, and the project serves both his and your various purposes, then you have a deal.

Balance the advantages with the risk. This ultimately is simply your judgement of the outside publisher's bona fides and intentions. Here the need to have had publishing experience is particularly apropos. If you haven't had that experience, then it would certainly be wise to take advice – and, with that aura which an institution has, it should not be difficult to get advice.

A cooperative venture starts in one of two ways; the library goes to the publisher, or the publisher comes to the library. In the former case, at the Library of Congress we have to be careful to see that notice of a particular proposal is posted widely (for we must not give the impression that we are in the business of making 'sweetheart deals'). An example was a manuscript (representing work paid for out of Library funds) which we were saddled with, and which we felt unable to publish. The next move was to go to our joint committee on printing to seek permission to go to an outside publisher – permission which was granted – and from there to canvass possible publishers. We found one that was interested; the project is published, the Library gets its royalty, and everyone (publisher included) is happy. In the case of a publisher approach, there is a difference; the Library has an obligation to cooperate with publishers, as it has an obligation to provide services for readers. Let us look at some examples of the projects that have resulted from these approaches.

1. Abrams wanted to produce a book drawing on all the Library's collections. A number of ideas were discussed before we finally hit upon the 'Treasures'

theme. A complicated deal was struck: the author was a retired member of staff who could write, to a deadline and to the required space, and who could help with picture research; Abrams paid him royalties and have a contract with him; Abrams were also going to have a contract with the Library, but at the last moment the Librarian asked for this to be converted into a 'letter of gift' instead – an Abrams 'thank-offering'; Abrams paid a lot of money doing special photography and on the production itself; the end-result has sold well, over 30,000 copies to date. Result again; everyone happy. The library has a fine book about its collection and a considerable income from it at no risk; the publisher has a good seller and recoups his substantial investment.

2. A publisher wanted to bring out an edition of the original 1897 guide to the Library, with new illustrations (the publisher took the photos). This was an example of enthusiastic cooperation with the publisher, and it worked well. In this case, there was no contract.

3. Publishers are encouraged to come and take a look at what is in the collections. A recent example is someone coming from Braziller, and then becoming keen to do a facsimile edition of Hiroshige's sketchbook – which is fine, as far as the Library is concerned.

4. Occasionally there are approaches from people other than publishers. If the approach comes from a corporation, it is one that should not be missed. In our own case, the American Folk Life Center wanted to put on a monster exhibit on a particular theme utilising the holdings of the Library – *The American Cowboy*. Sponsorship was sought and gained; United Technologies believed it would give them welcome publicity and prestige. At the same time they prefered to give away books rather than anything else, and the result was that the full upfront costs of producing the catalogue (over $100,000) came from them. The production was as complicated geographically as it was expensive – with the Curator in Santa Fe, editorial department in Washington, designer in the UK, setters in the UK, and printers in Baltimore – but it worked. And the Library did not have to put any money into it.

Kenneth Carpenter

Operating a microform publishing programme

A library's microform publishing programme is the result of a realisation that its collections have more than simply local significance. The programme is a microform one because it is the only economical way of achieving large-scale coverage. If the holdings of other libraries are brought together, something new is created, something that gives excellent possibilities and opportunities to researchers (possibilities that they are not always fast to take advantage of).

In the case of Harvard, and no doubt it is true of other libraries, there are other motives behind our efforts. In the first place, there is the preservation motive. Then there is the prospect of financial return (and quite large sums of money can be made). There is the possibility of getting some cataloguing done. Finally there is a degree of enhanced prestige to be gained.

The ideal is for a library to get a publisher to produce uncatalogued fiches; the ideal for the publisher is to make money from the project. As a major cost for the publisher is finding the project, the library is immediately in a position to help lower the cost (by suggesting the project). The publisher's other costs are made up of marketing and production costs, and what one might call the 'filling in' costs (no library will necessarily have complete holdings on a particular subject, and the publisher will have to go to other libraries too).

Evidently, there are fixed costs and variable costs present in different proportions, according to the project. But the most desirable project is one that is carried out on the largest scale – both for the publisher, who is getting more for covering fixed costs, and is likely to be able to persuade more libraries to buy the larger projects, and for the library, too. There is a conflict, of course; the library is likely just to want coverage of the material in its own collections, while it is much more useful to the researcher to have material from elsewhere included.

My own view is that I want publishers to put together the best package for the scholarly world; at the same time I want to make as much money as possible for my own library. I actually *want* to establish those 'sweetheart deals' – because there is so much involved that won't be covered in the contract. In a programme lasting 8 years, for example, one has got to be flexible. The basic conflict that is there can be overcome if 'fair play' rules; having said which, I must also say that not all publishers can be relied upon to keep to any rules.

In setting up a project, take the following into consideration always:

1. Money should always be exchanged.
2. Make sure that the library gets a copy of the published project (something that is quite often forgotten).
3. Pin your publisher down to a schedule.
4. Look into the nature of the bibliographical work required; the library must do its share.
5. Establish what happens to the master copies if the publishing firm fails.
6. Ensure that all are clear that there should be no avoidable damage to books (some damage is inevitable).
7. The library should be able to approve (and veto) all advertising material (something that publishers, who never look at a contract once it is signed, tend to forget).
8. Be clear whether a lack of orders will stop publication at any stage.
9. Do you want to ask for royalties in kind? This can stretch royalties by 30 to 40 per cent in my experience.
10. Where is the filming going to be carried out?

Discussion

DANA PRATT: Are publishers allowed to film on-site?

KENNETH CARPENTER: Yes.

D.P.: At the Library of Congress we have a photographic service, and they insist on doing all this type of work. I think it is probably more helpful if one can be flexible about this.

RUTH ANN STEWART: I have had experience of working with several different publishers and I have found that each have their own working arrangements. Sometimes we allow them in to film, otherwise our own photographic service does the work (which most publishers don't in fact like). You can ask quite a lot from microform publishers in terms of royalties, because their profit margin is quite high. In one case, a publisher even paid the salary of an archivist for 9 months, to organise a collection for photographing. Don't be shy about negotiating. Try for a rising royalty rate, for example; remember that in most cases, when a publisher has sold 10 or 20 sets of microfiches he has covered his costs, and after that he's on to a bestseller. Another possible scheme is to get publishers to look at your master-negative list and then put together a package; this is a marketing arrangement which can bring in a high royalty.

CLIVE FIELD: There is much more resistance to microform publications in the UK than there is in the USA, not only from readers, but from libraries too. No doubt this seems inexplicable to Americans here, but it is true. A lot of librarians are sceptical of micropublishers, having the attitude that once published in this way, particularly on a large scale, control of a collection is lost to the four winds. In a sense they feel that they are cutting their own throats; 'the rare books division is becoming a warehouse'.

K.C.: Harvard Business School filmed all their collections, and actually there wasn't a decline. If anything the reverse was true; the collections became more attractive, and scholars (who don't want to spend all their time wading through microfilm) were still coming. One should not forget the larger need, to disseminate material for research. We do it for books, after all, and we should do it for microfilm.

C.F.: I agree that it is a source of additional revenue that shouldn't be turned away. But the battles are with the library profession itself.

D.P.: I lament the attitude that one loses control of the collections. The library should ensure that it retains control. For example, when Chadwyck-Healey came to produce some large programmes of material in the Library of Congress, we ensured that we maintained full bibliographical control.

DR KARL DACHS: Turning to outside publishers in general; our own procedure is to go to publishers with particular projects, deliberating on which one we consider best for disseminating that project to the widest public. At the same time, publishers also come to us, if they learn that a particular catalogue is being prepared, for example. We are obliged to speak to all of them. In my experience the terms they offer vary considerably; one will provide you with 40 or 50 copies, another will provide a production subsidy of 10,000 DM.

MICHAEL HOARE: I agree with this approach. 'Choose horses for courses' is the motto one might adopt. All publishers are different, and it really must depend on the type of publication that is being planned. A problem is the terror of public servants of spending money in the private sector. This can make it difficult for libraries.

When drawing up agreements, it is worth taking into consideration whether the material is being given on an exclusive basis, or for a fixed period of exclusivity. This is particularly important for libraries, whose property is 'public'. Equally, consider the conditions for termination of the contract, and the circumstances in which the licence reverts to the library. It is also very useful to have a clause in the contract stating that 'should the contract pass out of the hands of the publisher, the terms may be re-negotiated'. After all, publishers do change hands, frequently.

R.A.S.: Try if you can to place the burden of copyright violation possibilities on to the publisher.

HUGH COBBE: We find it is useful to have a standard microfilm publishing contract; it is often chopped around, according to the particular project, but the framework is there.

D.P.: We cannot give any publisher an exclusive right over any material. But in practice it doesn't matter very much, because once something has been done it is unlikely that anyone else will do it.

H.C.: Our government at present is certainly very happy for us to be doing deals with the private sector. Competitions are held, and the highest bidder will win, so it is not really possible to do 'sweetheart deals', even if we wanted to.

ROBERT CROSS: Always give yourself the right (for example with artwork) to take copies for scholarly purposes, while giving publishers the right to reproduce it.

H.C.: The problem otherwise is that one becomes inhibited from photographing one's own material.

R.C.: And publishers are prepared to read the contract – when it suits them.

ALEC BOLTON: Would if be fair to say that the Library of Congress is becoming more of a packager than a publisher of general books?

D.P.: Certainly, when one is working with other publishers, this does affect your own publishing. It is unavoidable. One always has to consider whether one has the marketing strength needed to publish successfully any particular book.

M.H.: There is a middle course – the joint imprint.

D.P.: That certainly should not be forgotten. In the case of our *American Cowboy* catalogue, Harper & Row brought out the hardbound edition. It is interesting to notice the price differential – $50 as against $18.95 for our paperback edition – which represents in great part the cost of marketing, royalty to us, and discounts to the trade.

JANE CARR: For a 'Treasures' book, which is so key in giving a public image to an institution, wouldn't you have wanted your name on the cover somewhere?

D.P.: The absence of a joint imprint in this instance was due to the change that I mentioned, from a contract to a letter. Since we had that experience, the administration of the Library has become more flexible, so that the *American Cowboy* book, for instance, does have a joint imprint.

J.C.: My feeling is that such a book should help one's own list, which otherwise remains no easier to sell.

R.A.S.: Interestingly, we are at present doing a 'Treasures of the NYPL' with Abrams. It is the result of long negotiation. We have settled on a straight royalty arrangement; all the investment comes from Abrams, and it is very much their book. I don't believe they would have negotiated on terms of a joint imprint arrangement.

J.C.: Might a joint imprint in fact help them?

R.A.S.: With lesser publishers, maybe, but Abrams is enough of a name not to need that cachet.

D.P.: After our experience of working with corporations, can I urge you to try it yourselves. The costs of a large exhibit and catalogue are very high, after all. At the same time, keep your eyes wide open. The corporation's ultimate aim is publicity; so that such questions as the placing of the names on the catalogue can cause real tension.

M.H.: For UK institutions, it is a bit different, owing to differences in our tax laws. A company will only consider backing an exhibition if it is able to write off the cost against advertising (ie an overhead). As a charitable donation, simply, it would be liable to corporation tax. It is for this reason that the performing arts in the UK find it easier to raise money than the static arts.

D.P.: In fact United Technologies gifted the cost of the exhibit itself, but set the cost of the catalogue against the advertising budget.

ANN MATHESON: Returning to microfilming, does the Library of Congress insist that all the filming be done on the premises?

D.P.: Yes, all of it.

R.A.S.: At the NYPL we do let material out for filming, largely because no curatorial supervision is possible on the premises.

D.P.: I find this surprising; it can certainly produce problems if there is a disaster.

A.M.: The National Library of Scotland is certainly very reluctant to let any material out.

NICOLAS BARKER: You have to balance the individual factors in any case. There probably shouldn't be a magic embargo on material leaving the building. In the British Library, for example, a large quantity of material is going out for binding each year; the same factors are at play.

STEPHEN GREEN: Could one weigh the pros and cons of having a flat fee arrangement with a microform publisher as against a royalty over a number of years?

K.C.: In our view, a royalty offers a better return over a long period. But of course it is not always possible to get a royalty (for example a project that has been going on for a long time on a flat fee basis).

DAVID HALL: A barter arrangement is also worth considering. The Cambridge University Library agreement provides four frames of microfilm free of charge for every one that it puts in. It means that the Library is getting an important microfilm collection on advantageous terms.

R.A.S: At the NYPL, microform publishing used to be seen as part of preservation, and credit was given against the purchase of material from the micropublisher's catalogue. But this was a very difficult system to manage, and not one that I would ever recommend. A royalty arrangement is much easier to handle.

H.C.: We regard it as impracticable and unfair on the publisher to insist on a royalty where the British Library is providing only a moderate proportion of the material.

K.C.: In our case it is 50 per cent; after that we ask for a royalty.

JOANNA DODSWORTH: We sometimes demand a fee on publication – as with other reproduction rights.

M.H.: I would always go for a royalty (with money upfront as an advance). But remember that publishers' royalty departments are never the most efficient part of the publishing house, for obvious reasons. So, do chase up those royalties; make a diary entry to remind yourself when they are due – particularly for those which are part of a complicated contract, or are due from one of the smaller publishers that find it difficult to cope with royalties!

D.P.: Perhaps our watchword should be 'Be alert'!

Peter Haigh

Operating a translation journal publishing programme

In 1957, when Sputnick was first launched, it was realised that material published in Russian journals was not readily available to western readers. Accordingly the Russians were approached by the then National Lending Library for Science and Technology and a translation journal programme, the core of the present service operated by the British Library Lending Division, was initiated. There were no copyright restrictions – only agreement with the Americans as to who was to translate what. Since then, in America the programme has been taken over by commercial publishers; in this country the Lending Division arranges joint contracts with subject specialists and learned societies.

The arrangement shows well the economics of journal publishing; in comparison with the varying cash flow common in book publishing, such a programme benefits from the ability to obtain a high proportion of the sales revenue in advance of production. It is quite usual, for example, to have received 50 per cent of the revenue for a journal before the Russian journal has arrived, and at least six months before the translation is published. This revenue pattern is naturally very beneficial to the Library.

The actual programme has changed over the years; some journals prove more successful than others, subjects of interest change, new journals come onto the scene. A hoped-for steady flow of new journals has never really happened, and the programme has stayed at around ten journals. The service is augmented by the production of abstracts, and subscribers are able to request translations of particular articles. Annual subscriptions are anything up to £350 pa, with runs in the range of 300 to 800. The programme represents a very considerable source of revenue for the Library.

Nicolas Barker

Publishing and preservation

It might be said that I have seen the light. After 30 years of wasted life in publishing, manufacturing many millions of conservation problems – hot-glue paperbacks, for example, which fell to pieces within a decade – I am now redeeming my ill-spent youth by tackling the British Library's conservation problems.

Let me state at the outset that the Library does have an enormous conservation problem. First, out of a collection of over 10 million books, it is estimated that 12 per cent are actively in need of repair. When I joined the Library in 1976, the resources for coping with conservation were not inconsiderable – three (now two) binderies, with facilities for going outside to suitably trained commercial suppliers. However, all that could be done was to step up the level of repair to a point at which we were not actually falling back. The second part of the problem is that the surroundings in which the book stock is kept are appalling; it is at the mercy of a city's atmospheric pollution and out-housed storage for many books necessitates a good deal of moving to and fro. Conditions like this make preventive preservation extremely difficult.

The first aspect to the link between publishing and preservation is to be seen in the possibilities offered by micropublishing. In a sense, all the photographic resources used by a library are a form of publishing. It is the middle area of the demands placed on photographic departments that troubles me; whether it is photocopying or photography, books have to be handled. Photography is less of a worry, because time is taken over it. Photocopying – even if one is thankful that we are spared people making their own copies – remains a very great worry. The question is: what is the library itself getting from all this?

To my mind, the answer is 'very little', very little in fact except a bad bargain. All that can be done, and this is vital, is to monitor the activity, intervene where possible to prevent endless damage, and try to persuade people to accept microform – or hard-copy enlargements derived from microform.

Few would disagree that a library is in fact running a form of on-demand publishing service. And it doesn't take much ingenuity to turn this service into a full publishing programme. Let me take as an example the Library's Burney collection of (18th-century) newspapers. These had turned almost to pulp through years of over-use by researchers. A decision was made to microfilm the collection. And then the publishing possibilities presented themselves. In fact in the end Research Publications took the matter out of our hands, in the first of many such deals whereby the Library is provided with a much-needed master negative from which to meet photography demands, the opportunity to withdraw a collection from active use so that it can be conserved, as well as a tidy income from royalties.

The Library found that readers were largely sympathetic, and in return for the inconvenience that it knew was being caused it too tried to be sympathetic to individual pleas. The only protester was an institution which stated that it was 'appalled' by the Library's action, claiming that its work 'would be set back four years'. Apparently it would have preferred that the risk of the collection falling apart be taken. (The moral is always to ignore what readers say!)

The success of the Burney Collection microform project has led on to many larger-scale programmes. At present an extremely large programme is underway to microfilm all the Library's 18th-century books (an extension of the ESTC project). The sheer scale of the operation has necessitated a move outside the Library's own resources; Research Publications, the publishers, have set up (under Library supervision) an outside plant where all the filming is done. So far all has gone smoothly, and this success means that the Library – provided it is able to control transport and handling – is likely to remain sympathetic to requests to film off-premises. The great benefit of course is that the Library has an ever-increasing stock of books which have the protection of the microfilm back-up, and if the various projects continue on their present scale, this activity provides a major contribution to preventive preservation. For the fact remains that the British Library is one of the most used collections in the world, and for all that many of the books are 'physically exhausted' you cannot – as Museum conservators with their objects can – stop them being used.

The last element in the impact of conservation on publishing is yet to come. Here at the Library the idea grew for the introduction of a 'projection platemaker', a machine which will photograph the pages of books put in front of it, store up a sequential microfilm negative, and then print off at a size that enables copies of the book to be produced in hard copy. From this has come the idea to approach libraries with the offer of copies of the book photographed, printed and bound to a high standard, and at a reasonable price (it would be possible to produce an 8vo book of 480 pages at £5 a copy, on a 400 run). The essential thing would be that the library buys on subscription, to eliminate any stock problems and to ensure that costs are covered. If 200–400 subscribers could be found, we could start the first 'conservation book club'!

A final plea to library publishers: do as you would be done by. As manufacturing standards are falling, with a consequent lessening chance of survival for books now being published, it is very important that libraries themselves maintain high production standards. Alkaline paper need not cost more than other paper; try always to use it. Library binding costs more than other types of binding, but not that much more, so do specify it when you can. Offset the little extra that it will cost against the fact that you are not having to operate in the cut-throat commercial publishing world. It is self-interest, and self-interested simple measures such as these could well strengthen your publishing hand, as well as making the conservator's job a little bit easier.

Discussion

DANA PRATT: With reference to the Burney Collection. Why restore the newspapers, once the microfilming is done? Why not just store them?

NICOLAS BARKER: In this particular case, the newspapers are in large, tattered single sheets which must be restored, if they are to be touched again. And they will be touched again, for example by those engaged in watermark studies.

D.P.: The point to my question is that the Library of Congress has lovingly restored its own collection of 18th-century newspapers.

IAN GIBB: In this country, the Act of Parliament which set up the British Library states that we are not able to dispose of any pre-1850 material; morally, by implication, we are obliged to keep it. But quite apart from that, we don't really know how people actually make use of the Library's collections, at least in humanities subjects (it is easier with scientists), and we certainly cannot foresee how particular material will be studied in future years.

N.J.B.: Reducing the cost of preservation is vital. Before we say goodbye to books, the fact remains that a book is an immensely useful information tool. The sheer commonness of books is in a way their strength (although it makes people more cavalier when they handle them). And there is a staggering amount of archaeological evidence in books which has hardly been touched as yet.

DR GERAINT GRYFFYDD: It is certainly true that information can be obtained from microfilm. But always for textual criticism and bibliographical study it is the physical object itself that must be studied.

D.P.: I am worried about the cost equation of conservation. Are other institutions achieving the twin aims of conservation and dissemination?

JOANNA DODSWORTH: I would say that making photographs and filmstrips available has increased the number of people who come to the Bodleian and say that they 'need to see the original'. So in many ways dissemination only exacerbates the conservation problem.

N.J.B.: But at least it gives an option – 'no copy, no option'.

KENNETH CARPENTER: It can be cumbersome, and difficult for the users, when referred to a microform version, if what is available is in any way selective. It is the virtue of large-scale microform programmes that libraries can know straightaway what is actually available.

N.J.B.: It is fine, so long as everyone knows where they are.

HUGH COBBE: In the case of the Burney Papers, the British Library in fact took some of the commercial risk, by doing all the photography. In return, the Library received a larger royalty, and the publisher certainly looked at the project with more interest initially.

K.C.: My comment on the 'projection platemaker' is that there are a lot of books that don't deserve having 200 copies made, and it would probably be difficult to persuade people to take them. Then, for more modern material, copyright problems always intrude – and note that it is the more modern books which are having a shorter and shorter life and will be in need of such copying.

Hugh Pinnock

Aspects of new technology

'New technology' is a wide-ranging term, with many definitions. In the context in which I am speaking, I regard it to mean the handling of digitised information – inputting, manipulating, storing, transmitting and outputting. I shall take each of these processes in turn, giving an observer's view of the techniques involved and the possibilities that present themselves.

First, inputting. Whether it be the author or the editor or anyone else who actually performs the task, the essential means of inputting is by keyboarding. Usually this will be done on a microcomputer – and as we all know the prospects for the future rôle to be played by micros grow daily, as capability increases and price comes down. Micros are bound to offer an ever more powerful local editing capability as well as transmission capability for remote users; the major hurdle is still communications between machines, but compatibility is not necessarily the problem it once was. Dedicated word-processors are less in use because they are much more expensive. They are, however, a lot more sophisticated in their applications, with considerable power; their potential for bringing together an author's text and for networking is great, but the real advantage comes in the output produced. A third machine commonly used is the optical character reader (or digital facsimile machine). This allows an author to create material on a traditional typewriter, which is then 'read' and outputted in a different format (it also allows the text of books to be manipulated for a revised edition, without the need for re-keyboarding). The latest machines are a great improvement on their predecessors, being able to 'read' practically any typeface – although slowly – and the prospects are good, given the right applications. But the results of research (by the British Library and others) show that digital facsimile has a long way to go yet; it is fine for a business letter, but not for information handling, particularly where a dense text is involved.

Looking at new developments here, one can say that microcomputers are becoming increasingly 'user-friendly'; the latest software, for example, can enable an author to log forward and backward much more quickly than is generally the case. More and more software is being developed with a 'publishing' application in mind.

As for optical character readers, their potential for the manipulation of existing material ensures that they are of interest to librarians, although it is recognised that there is a long way to go. The British Library has in fact developed its own image digitiser. This treats the contents of each page as an image (in this way it is similar to a standard digital facsimile machine) but it also has the ability to scan the contents of each book without any heavy handling being involved – the book being opened only a few degrees. The machine, especially adapted for library use, is also much faster than a conventional model; an A4 page, for example, can be scanned in 5 seconds. The quality, too, is high, with readability down to 6 pt. faces. Resolution can be varied, and the machine can be connected to any kind of transmission device or printer. This is expected to retail at about £30,000 on the UK market.

Once the inputting is achieved, the next steps are manipulation and transmission (with floppy discs becoming the standard, storage is the least of the problems with the new technology – although one should always beware the relative ease with which stored material can suddenly be lost through error). The text can be transmitted on a number of different output media. There is paper, of course; here the quality of the printer (and printers vary greatly in quality, from the most basic dot-matrix to the most sophisticated daisy-wheel) is a prime consideration. There is also the storage problem related to large quantities of paper. There is microform, said to be permanent (but is it?), which can be read on readers, or converted to hard copy or can be re-converted to a digital system. In this context, the British Library is exploring the possibilities of microfiche carrels for readers, in which one will be able to access remotely, onto library catalogues, for example. The drawbacks are slowness and the difficulties of updating microfiche.

Turning to another commonly touted area of the new technology, videodiscs, one can say that up till now the greatest development has been in applications for the domestic entertainment market, with publishing applications scarcely considered. There is a danger therefore that if the domestic market runs out of steam (and there have been ominous signs of this) then the interesting (to us) publishing possibilities might do so too.

The essential point about the videodisc is that it has great storage capability, along with high-quality graphics. The information retrieval possibilities are what attract most, and the fact that the disc cannot record (the problem as far as domestic users are concerned) is of small moment.

Videodisc programmes are produced on videotape which is then put through a system whereby information is turned into light pulses on a laser, and a glass master originated. The disc itself has 14 billion 'pits' (enough for one hour), bringing it close to the wavelength of light. Recording errors, as can be imagined, have important implications. For playback, a laser is played onto the disc and a pattern is returned which reconstructs the material in video format on the monitor. The number of frames which can be produced varies according to the system: in the USA it is commonly 54,000, while in the UK it is 47,000 (per side). That is about 100,000 frames on one disc (in continuous play mode – the figure is reduced for information storage), which represents a lot of storage capacity. Coupled to this is the cheapness of videodiscs. There is the original production cost of course, but beyond this only the mastering process which costs $2,000 – 4,000, and copies at about $10 apiece. Videodiscs are also relatively robust and do not wear out.

As far as publishing is concerned, one can envisage the videodisc being the core of a computer-controllable information store of high quality. In the USA there has been much investment in research into the capability of storing in digital form, either recorded on-site at the computer or off a video. A technique has been developed for getting information in printed form burnt directly into a digital optical disc surface and checked immediately by computer (the DRAW – Direct Read After Write – system). The system has the advantages of high capacity (1 million characters per side) and low error rate. It has potential as a mass storage system (perhaps used on the jukebox principle). The disadvantage at present is the high cost – a cost that would diminish if large quantities of information were being fed through (in the case of a large electronic publisher, for example).

Research in the UK has tended to question the need for such systems. With a cheap video system, if one can get digitised text onto it then you have a dual-purpose use. We are a long way from seeing demonstrable systems, but this is the trend in present thinking.

Videodisc is already showing its potential as a high-speed graphic retrieval instrument. VideoPatsearch, available at the British Library, is an example – a hybrid system combining videodisc and online access. One can see all sorts of other possibilities; an illustrated manuscripts catalogue or encyclopaedia of medical techniques, perhaps. In comparisons of storage costs on videodisc and optical disc as against magnetic tape, the videodisc would seem to win. In terms of mass publication, the much cheaper videodisc will win over the optical disc. And then in comparison with microform, the videodisc cost per frame looks like being less (although this is balanced out by more expensive video display monitors and printers).

At the Library of Congress two applications have been explored. First, a sophisticated laserprinter to produce LC catalogue cards for the MARC system, printing on demand. This machine, developed by Xerox, is the basis of the laserprinters working commercially more and more commonly. Second, a system has been developed by which older handwritten and oriental language cards can be scanned digitally, and through image-enhancement technology imperfections (in this case water-staining) removed. The output is stored on optical disc. Eventually the Library will have the capability of publishing on demand 6 million catalogue cards.

Discussion

RUTH ANN STEWART: In the USA the publishers Abrams have created a videodisc of their book, *Treasures of the National Gallery of Art*. All sorts of royalty negotiations have been necessary, as there is no precedent to apply.

DR CLIVE FIELD: The key question is, have developments in technology stabilised enough to justify investment? Is there not a case for waiting longer?

HUGH PINNOCK: In a reference context, this is probably the sensible course. On the other hand, if your library operates an audio-visual service (where a videodisc for example is simply an alternative medium for output) then it's a different matter.

DANA PRATT: The next stage being worked on now is the possibility of interaction between a video and a microcomputer (commercial publishers are keenly exploring the educational potential for this).

THOMAS WRIGHT: How does all this relate to the printed book?

H.P.: It doesn't at the moment. But the next stages of digitising of information bring the electronic book closer.

MICHAEL HOARE: If we wanted to produce an inventory of, say, our collections of prints and drawings, on videodisc, what production costs are likely to be involved, beyond the photography itself?

H.P.: You would need to obtain estimates from potential suppliers – all I can say is that the more copies you can produce the better.

DR GERAINT GRYFFYDD: One potential application is reading at a distance. It seems to me that the technology that makes it possible is already here.

H.P.: In terms of publishing, the difficult thing is going to be to decide what to publish, rather than how to do it. There is a lot of room on a disc. It is likely that the large-scale projects will be the ones which make more sense.

D.P.: I particularly like the idea of a 1940s jukebox accessed into a 1980s videodisc, enabling one to gain quick access to records! If I could just add to what has been said about the Library of Congress catalogue card project; we are in fact exploring the possibilities of moving on to a larger project in which a digital optical disc is used for the storage of both text and illustrations. It is in an early stage as yet, and it is an uncharted area for anyone, with copyright being a central issue.

David Martin

Electronic publishing

'Library publishing' encompasses a very diverse cross-section of publications. I aim to focus on the forms of electronic publishing that at least some of us are involved with today.

I shall begin with an example of current database publishing, which happens to be close to home for me – the British Library's *British National Bibliography* operation (on MARC).

Fundamental to database publishing is the database computer file itself. From this central core a variety of products can be developed. In the case of *BNB*, there is:

1. Magnetic Tape (ie the MARC exchange tape service).

2. Printed publications (we are currently looking at the possibilities of producing these by laserprinter, in order to bypass the phototypesetting process).

3. Microfiche.

4. A card service, produced by laserprinter (which gives good quality).

5. A selective records service.

6. On-line retrieval (terminals give access to MARC and other files).

7. An option for users of (6) to do so via a telecommunications link.

This I think is a characteristic system, in which a variety of technologies are used to tailor information to different applications.

The cost profiles of each application are very different. At the centre is a large fixed cost – the larger cost that any on-line system involves. A key question in any publishing operation of this nature is the basis on which this central cost has to be recovered (if at all). For example, the database might represent the whole library catalogue, which the library feels it has to create in any case; here any contributions that come from marketing the database may not be so significant as they would be in a commercially-run operation. In the case of the British Library's MARC system, this is a type of hybrid; the information that goes onto the database is all part of the acquisitions cataloguing process, but because it is also a service for others information is added that would not have been needed if only for internal use.

The extent to which there is a policy of getting a return on the costs of the database colours the publishing approach adopted. First, the high fixed cost leads to complicated questions of what to charge for, and how to cost, different services. Secondly, there is the problem of declining print sales at the same time as there is increasing use by electronic users; there is likely to be a definite transition from the traditional media to electronic media. This complication only reinforces the view that one should ensure that all the services offered contribute to the central cost; if demand diminishes beyond a specified figure and a service offered is no longer cost-effective, then it should probably cease.

In terms of electronic 'publishing products' that the British Library currently offers, there are:

1. Complete machine-readable files.

2. Selected machine-readable files.

3. On-line access itself.

Now, if you provide (1), you are of course giving the customer the ability to do exactly what you yourself are doing – passing on a file to a third party. On-line access, such as is increasingly used, now makes it possible for records to be re-used on an intelligent microcomputer, and this inevitably creates a dilemma as far as copyright is concerned. British copyright law is grey about this, although in the USA it is in fact now possible to copyright a database. Traditionally the British Library has preferred to make use of an agreement setting out the terms on which the file is supplied, rather than rely on the vagaries of copyright law. This has worked well so long as distribution is confined to a comparatively limited number of institutions. But it begins to break down once computer systems become networked, and files are mixed with records created elsewhere. One has to think very hard about the conditions of use one would need to apply in a situation in which an inter-library network becomes very freely accessed; at present it is a central area of concern.

It is not just an area of concern for national bibliographic agencies. In publishing traditionally the publisher actively distributes his products to his customers; in database publishing, the reverse is true – it is the user at his terminal who takes the initiative, and it is the publisher who is more or less passive. The extent to which the publisher's product, his database, can go beyond his control, can be seen in the example of university libraries which develop their own on-line catalogue, then have it connected to a local area network; the logical extension is the setting up of a university national network (currently being set up in the UK), using technology which is identical to British Telecom's national packet-switch network, which in turn enables the database to go 'on-line' right across the world. The links are nearly all in place; the implications are there for all of us to consider.

Discussion

DANA PRATT: It might be said that those who produce databases are all, unwittingly, publishers.

RACHAEL GOLDSTEIN: One can speculate that many catalogues etc which are produced on-line are already accessible to other libraries.

D.P.: The Library of Congress NUC will now only be produced on microfiche, and already it is being called antique!

HUGH COBBE: It ought to be remembered, however, that there are huge library holdings which are still 'undigitised' (the British Library has only had its database since 1975, for example). The printed catalogue still has its place, and as databases take over our catalogues, the ease with which all sorts of printed catalogues can be derived from them will be dramatically increased.

DAVID MARTIN: The development of the Eighteenth Century Short Title Catalogue could only have come about in the way it has because of the systems that the participating libraries already had in place. But the situation in the UK is not mirrored by that in the USA – where there are a small number of well-established public utilities, and a significant movement to 'stand-alone systems', integrating all sorts of library functions but going against remote use.

DR GERAINT GRYFFYDD: What are the prospects of a UK library database system?

D.M.: The development of plans for linking databases in the UK is well in hand, although there is no plan for a centralised utility.

H.C.: In British Library Reference Division, our specialised databases (ESTC for example) are regarded as a valuable property – they certainly represent a huge investment – which we should like to exploit in any way we can. Unfortunately this fits in none too well with the Library policy in other areas, in which services are offered for nominal amounts; problems can therefore be caused.

D.P.: It all needs to be planned with the proper technical support (RLIN in the case of the ESTC project for example). The fundamental question to return to internally is the proportion of the database costs that need to be recovered, as this must be the main factor in shaping one's policy in marketing the products obtainable from it.

DR CLIVE FIELD: Can I ask if ESTC will be available on magnetic tape, as well as on microfiche?

H.C.: It will be eventually. It is of course available on-line now, but we must consider the protection it needs as a 'property' for the time being.

Hugh Cobbe

Summing-up

The time has come to sum up the seminar. When I first thought of the idea, I have to confess that I was not at all sure either what the response would be or, even if the response was good, whether in fact it would prove useful to, and fulfil the expectations of, the participants in the event.

I have to say that I am most encouraged by what has taken place. The discussion has been continuous, and has not, as can so often happen on these occasions, been unduly dominated by a small group of speakers leaving a large silent majority either scribbling on their note-pads or looking at the ceiling! My impression has been that all the participants have found the presentations and the substance of the discussions more or less relevant to their own experience.

In this connection my decision that the number of participants should be strictly limited (this was making a virtue of necessity because the truth of the matter is that the fire regulations forbid more than 50 people meeting in this room) has proved, in my view, to have been the correct one. The fact that we have all been able to sit around a table has, I am certain, contributed to the freedom of discussion.

I think that the major point to emerge throughout the first day's proceedings was the need for professionalism in our publishing activities, whether we are talking about editorial, production or marketing matters. That means in effect either recruiting from the publishing industry or turning home-grown specimens, like myself, into publishers by sending them on suitable training courses.

Another point was that we must keep up with technology, both of the traditional and newer electronic kinds, in order to print effectively.

We must watch our finances, for in the kinds of institution where we work financial criteria can become blurred; this does not mean that we apply rigorous financial criteria of performance to our ventures but that we ensure that we are aware of true costs and true market values of our products.

Yesterday we became clear that, when we 'get into bed' with the private sector we must be aware of the perspectives and objectives of that sector in order to ensure that we 'get the best deal'. Here again, publishing expertise is important in order to monitor what our private sector partners are up to. As far as financial arrangements of such partnerships go, I think there was a spectrum of requirement ranging from, on the one hand, those of us who tend to avoid doing, either by rule or inclination, what could be done more efficiently by the private sector and who were disinclined to look for significant financial return on the grounds that any such return was of no direct benefit to the institution, to, on the other hand, those of us who – with revenue targets to meet in order not to endanger other activities of our institution – will soak our partners for everything we can get! It is also clear that there are many of us who are restricted by rules and regulations, for example to prevent corruption, in our dealings with the private sector.

I think that we were all agreed that publication, by whatever means, was an important instrument for making the collections of our institutions better known; in fact this was as important a reason for a publishing programme as the earning of revenue.

We also agreed that the publication of material in our collections, especially in microform, was of direct benefit to our preservation programmes and I think that some further consultation will be taking place on arrangements with microform publishers.

We looked at what new technology is coming along and how it might apply to our publishing policies, and finally at the particular problems and challenges of the computer network as an instrument of publication.

The level of discussion stayed on a fairly general level as we examined each facet of the publishing operation and I think that it is here that I have a slight regret. I went last year to a conference of small European academic and scholarly presses, where a whole session was devoted to a series of case studies. Generalisation about publishing is of course a distillation of the lessons learnt on the ground and I firmly believe that there is no substitute for practical experience in our profession. Six pages of particular cases are worth one generalisation.

Accordingly I should like to have heard, now I come to look back on the seminar, many more accounts of interesting cases from our communal experience of both publishing ourselves or making deals with others who do so. If such a seminar takes place again I would strongly urge that a session or two is included along the lines of a clinic, for we can learn more from each other's successes and mistakes than from a whole raft of well-turned papers!

And it is at this point that we should turn to look into the future. There is no doubt that this seminar has proved worthwhile, and if only one thing happens in the field of library publishing which would not have happened if this seminar had not taken place, then it will have proved downright valuable. We in the British Library feel that much of the future of libraries depends on cooperation, and this must apply in this field as in others.

Let us look briefly at the various segments of the publishing operation and see what the options are.

First, there is the subject matter of publications. Someone said yesterday that a microform publication of a collection in a library is a good thing, but a microform publication of a collection in three or four libraries is even better. The same could be said of catalogues, and here perhaps there is some potential for getting together (although it wasn't actually said yesterday, I think that it was felt, and it is certainly my opinion, that the publication of microform collections is best left to microform publishers – they present marketing problems of a very special kind – but the same is not necessarily true of catalogues); from time to time exhibitions go touring (we are sending one to the Getty Museum and on to the Pierpont Morgan Library later this year) and there is then an opportunity for a joint publication of the catalogue. And this will apply to other types of publication too.

Cooperation in terms of production is difficult; even in the big world outside, co-publishers will usually leave production matters to just one of the partners, but where there is a joint interest in a book, then the print-run which is made possible by two outlets will reduce the cost per copy for both. There is no reason, on the face of it, why libraries should not join up as co-publishers, provided plenty of time (and I mean plenty) is left for ratification of any arrangements by all the committees involved!

There are of course many opportunities in the field of marketing and it is likely that this will prove a fruitful topic for further discussion. Finally we can consider each other's product for sale in bookshops, where we have them. I feel hesitant about suggesting this since, at the moment, we do not have our own book-stall and so are not in a position to make reciprocal arrangements, but when the time comes and the British Library begins to occupy its new building at St Pancras, we shall have a sales area and, given the fact that we do not expect the tourist to beat a path to our door – despite the Magna Carta and the Lindisfarne Gospels – all at once, I think that there is something to be said for turning the shop we have there into a mecca for people who want to buy bibliographies, catalogues and the other manifestations of library publishing. This, however, is for the future.

Of course, one factor which militates against joint ventures in publishing between libraries can be incompatibility of financial systems. For example, I should very much like to find something which the Library of Congress and the British Library could publish together, but, as with computers, I am afraid that I don't think that our financial systems could be made to talk to one another!

These then are all matters for us to discuss in the remaining part of this seminar and afterwards, but perhaps the point we should look at first is whether there is a continuing value for such meetings as this. I am very aware that the library profession is one in which international committees are set up at the drop of an agenda paper; I am also aware that the more institutionalised such committees become, the less they achieve, and the more time is spent on international diplomatic manoeuvring. But hearing that in mind, do people think that there should be, some time in the future, another seminar, and if so, how would it be as useful as this without covering the same ground all over again? I have indicated one mode of procedure that I feel was not adequately explored this time, but that is only one. I open the discussion.

Discussion:
a summary

The first subject considered was whether it was worthwhile meeting together again as a group, and if so, when. There was unanimous agreement that there would be profit in a regular biennial conference, possibly timed to take place shortly before or after the Frankfurt Book Fair. Various titles for the group were considered (including Dana Pratt's suggestion of the 'Metaxa Brandy Group', to give a suitable air of informality), agreement then being reached on the name 'International Group of Publishing Libraries'. Members would be research libraries to which visitors came from a distance, and which had or wished to have an active publishing programme. A small working party was established to undertake the preparations for a second conference. To Gwynneth Evans's point that the seminar had tended to stay away from publishing policy matters as such, Hugh Cobbe replied that he considered these to be the proper concern of a more broadly assembled group of librarians; this forum was really one in which specifically publishing questions were discussed. Kenneth Carpenter agreed that the seminar had focused on 'how to get it published', and wondered if in the future the larger possibilities of fostering cooperative bibliographical ventures might be considered, a suggestion strongly endorsed by Nicolas Barker, who pointed to the fact that compiling bibliographies was nowadays beyond the resources of individuals and had to be a team effort. There were already several such projects (for example, ESTC and ISTC); it was agreed that discussion of other possible cooperative projects could well be valuable, but considered from a publishing rather than a library resource point of view.

Discussion then moved on to the opportunities that there were for practical immediate cooperation between publishing libraries. If co-publication proved impossible (and it was certainly something that several participants were keen to pursue), at least libraries could send each other their publications lists, investigate the possibilities of shared mailings and pooling of resources on mailing lists, in order to be more effective in marketing internationally. The point was made that many commercial mailing lists were simply much larger than required; it was the specialist lists, such as individual libraries (and other bodies, such as the Association of American University Presses) had built up, which were likely to be the most useful. As for other marketing possibilities, there was discussion as to whether it might be possible to combine in appointing an agent for all the libraries' lists in a particular market, for example Japan; there was, however, some scepticism as to the ease with which such an agency might be set up, and there was the problem that no one agent was likely to be suitable to carry such a variety of lists.

Other suggestions for cooperation included a request for exchanges of posters advertising exhibitions; displays of catalogues from other libraries; joint representation at trade fairs; sharing of budget manipulation expertise. There was also a suggestion that the group be broken into smaller units to discuss specific subjects, for example merchandising or journals.

The seminar ended with the hope expressed that as many as possible who were present and several who had not been able to come would reassemble in 1985 to repeat what all had considered to have been a very valuable meeting.